The New York Criminal Statute Handbook

for use with

Sue Titus Reid's

Criminal Law
Seventh Edition

Steven J. Dunker
Northeastern State University

Research Assistants
Jennifer Zachry
Marisa Patrick

New York Oxford
Oxford University Press
2008

Oxford University Press, Inc., publishes works that further Oxford University's objective of excellence in research, scholarship, and education.

Oxford New York
Auckland Cape Town Dar es Salaam Hong Kong Karachi
Kuala Lumpur Madrid Melbourne Mexico City Nairobi
New Delhi Shanghai Taipei Toronto

With offices in
Argentina Austria Brazil Chile Czech Republic France Greece
Guatemala Hungary Italy Japan Poland Portugal Singapore
South Korea Switzerland Thailand Turkey Ukraine Vietnam

Published by Oxford University Press, Inc.
198 Madison Avenue, New York, New York 10016
http://www.oup.com

ISBN 978-0-19-533238-4

Printing number: 9 8 7 6 5 4 3 2 1

Printed in the United States of America
on acid-free paper

Table of Contents

Preface

Framework of This Statute Handbook

The New York statutes in this book have been arranged following the outline of Sue Titus Reid's *Criminal Law*, Seventh Edition textbook. You should read the corresponding chapter in the textbook before beginning each chapter in this guide on the statutes. Dr. Reid's text does a good job explaining the concepts behind each area of law. This manual includes additional comments when they are appropriate in order to further explain how the state statute works. At the end of each chapter, there are scenario questions you can use to test your knowledge and understanding of the statutes in each chapter.

Acknowledgments

I wish to thank my wife Kristie and my children Kylie, Chris, Parker, Russell, and Patrick for their understanding and patience while I wrote this book.

I also wish to thank my research assistant Jennifer Zachry for all of her help. I am indebted to Sue Titus Reid, as well as Claude Teweles, Nina Hickey, and Scott Carter at Roxbury Publishing Company for putting up with all the issues caused by a first-time author.

—Steven J. Dunker
November 2006

Chapter 1
An Introduction to New York Criminal Statutes

Due to their widespread distribution, criminal law textbooks must address topics by thoroughly examining all the legal concepts about a particular point of law. They often explore the alternative laws available for use by the state and federal governments. For example, most textbooks discuss the various insanity tests and go far beyond the process selected by New York. This book follows Dr. Reid's treatment of the criminal law. Each chapter here provides the relevant New York statutes corresponding with the topics in the textbook.

In our dual court system each state and the federal government develops their own set of criminal law statutes. Sometimes these statutes mirror those of other states, at other times they may be unique. Terminology may also vary. You might not find a statute for your state that corresponds with a law discussed in the text, especially concerning some of the innovative defenses.

I. Sources of Criminal Law

New York bases its criminal law on four sources: statutory law, judicial decisions (case law), administrative law, and the federal and state Constitutions. The majority of criminal law is statute driven. States enact statutes to govern a particular issue. To be convicted of a violation of a criminal law you must either commit some forbidden act or fail to take an action that is required by law. Most of New York's criminal law derives from statutes.

A statute is an act of the legislature to declare, command, or prohibit something. It is to be distinguished from concurrent resolutions of the senate and assembly, and also from the local enactments of cities, towns, and villages.

II. New York Statute Citations

A "citation" uniquely identifies a legal document. In this book, you will see many citations to criminal statutes. We use these citations to locate and identify laws.

Consider for a moment that a citation is the "address" of a statute. If you are given the street address of 123 Main Street, you can use the address to locate that exact spot. A citation is the same way. You use a citation to locate the exact statute it is referring to. An example of a New York statute citation is: "New York Penal Law § 221.05 Unlawful possession of marihuana."

Reading a New York Citation

You "read" a citation in the following way:

Example: "New York Penal Law § 221.05 Unlawful possession of marihuana"

New York:	The source of the laws.
Penal Law:	The chapter of New York laws that concerns criminal law.

§ 221.05: The article number and statute number.
Unlawful possession of marihuana: A description of the statute.

In some publications you may see a statute number proceeded by the symbol "§". The symbol "§" stands for "section."

III. Classification of Crimes

New York crimes are classified as *felonies*, *misdemeanors*, *violations*, and *traffic infractions*. The focus of this book is on felonies and misdemeanors. The following New York statutes define the four types of crimes and list their classifications.

§ 55.10 Designation of offenses.

1. Felonies.

(a) The particular classification or subclassification of each felony defined in this chapter is expressly designated in the section or article defining it.

(b) Any offense defined outside this chapter which is declared by law to be a felony without specification of the classification thereof, or for which a law outside this chapter provides a sentence to a term of imprisonment in excess of one year, shall be deemed a class E felony.

2. Misdemeanors.

(a) Each misdemeanor defined in this chapter is either a class A misdemeanor or a class B misdemeanor, as expressly designated in the section or article defining it.

(b) Any offense defined outside this chapter which is declared by law to be a misdemeanor without specification of the classification thereof or of the sentence therefor shall be deemed a class A misdemeanor.

(c) Except as provided in paragraph (b) of subdivision three, where an offense is defined outside this chapter and a sentence to a term of imprisonment in excess of fifteen days but not in excess of one year is provided in the law or ordinance defining it, such offense shall be deemed an unclassified misdemeanor.

3. Violations. Every violation defined in this chapter is expressly designated as such. Any offense defined outside this chapter which is not expressly designated a violation shall be deemed a violation if:

(a) Notwithstanding any other designation specified in the law or ordinance defining it, a sentence to a term of imprisonment which is not in excess of fifteen days is provided therein, or the only sentence provided therein is a fine; or

(b) A sentence to a term of imprisonment in excess of fifteen days is provided for such offense in a law or ordinance enacted prior to the effective date of this chapter but the offense was not a crime prior to that date.

4. Traffic infraction. Notwithstanding any other provision of this section, an offense which is defined as a "traffic infraction" shall not be deemed a violation or a misdemeanor by virtue of the sentence prescribed therefor.

§ 55.05 Classifications of felonies and misdemeanors.

1. Felonies. Felonies are classified, for the purpose of sentence, into five categories as follows:

(a) Class A felonies;

(b) Class B felonies;

(c) Class C felonies;

(d) Class D felonies; and

(e) Class E felonies.

Class A felonies are subclassified, for the purpose of sentence, into two categories as follows: subclass I and subclass II, to be known as class A-I and class A-II felonies, respectively.

2. Misdemeanors. Misdemeanors are classified, for the purpose of sentence, into three categories as follows:

(a) Class A misdemeanors;

(b) Class B misdemeanors; and

(c) Unclassified misdemeanors.

§ 20.10 Geographical jurisdiction of offenses; definitions of terms.

The following definitions are applicable to this article:

1. "This state" means New York State as its boundaries are prescribed in the state law, and the space over it.

2. "County" means any of the sixty-two counties of this state as its boundaries are prescribed by law, and the space over it.

3. "Result of an offense." When a specific consequence, such as the death of the victim in a homicide case, is an element of an offense, the occurrence of such consequence constitutes the "result" of such offense. An offense of which a result is an element is a "result offense."

4. "Particular effect of an offense." When conduct constituting an offense produces consequences which, though not necessarily amounting to a result or element of such offense, have a materially harmful impact upon the governmental processes or community welfare of a particular jurisdiction, or result in the defrauding of persons in such jurisdiction, such conduct and offense have a "particular effect" upon such jurisdiction.

Questions

1. Mike is sentenced to one year. Based on the statutes in this chapter, did he commit a felony or a misdemeanor?

2. John is sentenced to two years incarceration in the state prison and a fine of $1,000 for possession of drugs. Has he been convicted of a felony or a misdemeanor?

2. Mary is waiting to be sentenced for a "Class A" misdemeanor. Based on the information in this chapter, what is the greatest amount of jail time she can get?

Chapter 2
Elements of a Crime

It is generally recognized that for a crime to occur there needs to be a voluntary act or a failure to act, along with a criminal intent. This is sometimes regarded as the requirements of *actus reus* and *mens rea*. For most criminal violations, New York requires both a criminal act and a criminal intent.

I. A Criminal Act (*Actus Reus*)

Comment: A defendant must either perform a voluntary act or fail to perform a legally required action that he or she had the ability to perform. Possession alone is not considered an act, unless the defendant is aware or should be aware that he or she exercised control over the item. Section 15.00 defines the legal definitions surrounding the criminal act.

§ 15.00 Culpability; definitions of terms.

The following definitions are applicable to this chapter:

1. "Act" means a bodily movement.

2. "Voluntary act" means a bodily movement performed consciously as a result of effort or determination, and includes the possession of property if the actor was aware of his physical possession or control thereof for a sufficient period to have been able to terminate it.

3. "Omission" means a failure to perform an act as to which a duty of performance is imposed by law.

4. "Conduct" means an act or omission and its accompanying mental state.

5. "To act" means either to perform an act or to omit to perform an act.

6. "Culpable mental state" means "intentionally" or "knowingly" or "recklessly" or with "criminal negligence," as these terms are defined in section 15.05.

II. A Criminal Intent (*Mens Rea*)

Comment: Under New York law, *mens rea* is required unless the offense statute clearly states that absolute liability is to be imposed. Like the Model Penal Code, New York has four levels of mental culpability, and has opted not to use the mental state of "purposely." Instead, the highest mental state is that of "intentionally." The state follows the traditional definitions concerning the mental states of *knowingly*, *recklessly*, and *negligence*. Generally, for criminal offenses, the legislature only punishes acts that are intentionally committed.

§ 15.05 Culpability; definitions of culpable mental states.

The following definitions are applicable to this chapter:

1. "Intentionally." A person acts intentionally with respect to a result or to conduct described by a statute defining an offense when his conscious objective is to cause such result or to engage in such conduct.

2. "Knowingly." A person acts knowingly with respect to conduct or to a circumstance described by a statute defining an offense when he is aware that his conduct is of such nature or that such circumstance exists.

3. "Recklessly." A person acts recklessly with respect to a result or to a circumstance described by a statute defining an offense when he is aware of and consciously disregards a substantial and unjustifiable risk that such result will occur or that such circumstance exists. The risk must be of such nature and degree that disregard thereof constitutes a gross deviation from the standard of conduct that a reasonable person would observe in the situation. A person who creates such a risk but is unaware thereof solely by reason of voluntary intoxication also acts recklessly with respect thereto.

4. "Criminal negligence." A person acts with criminal negligence with respect to a result or to a circumstance described by a statute defining an offense when he fails to perceive a substantial and unjustifiable risk that such result will occur or that such circumstance exists. The risk must be of such nature and degree that the failure to perceive it constitutes a gross deviation from the standard of care that a reasonable person would observe in the situation.

§ 15.15 Construction of statutes with respect to culpability requirements.

1. When the commission of an offense defined in this chapter, or some element of an offense, requires a particular culpable mental state, such mental state is ordinarily designated in the statute defining the offense by use of the terms "intentionally," "knowingly," "recklessly" or "criminal negligence," or by use of terms, such as "with intent to defraud" and "knowing it to be false," describing a specific kind of intent or knowledge. When one and only one of such terms appears in a statute defining an offense, it is presumed to apply to every element of the offense unless an intent to limit its application clearly appears.

2. Although no culpable mental state is expressly designated in a statute defining an offense, a culpable mental state may nevertheless be required for the commission of such offense, or with respect to some or all of the material elements thereof, if the proscribed conduct necessarily involves such culpable mental state. A statute defining a crime, unless clearly indicating a legislative intent to impose strict liability, should be construed as defining a crime of mental culpability. This subdivision applies to offenses defined both in and outside this chapter.

III. Strict Liability

Comment: Exceeding the speed limit is one of the clearest examples of an absolute liability violation. The state does not have to prove a mental state to achieve a conviction. Without any type of *mens rea* argument, a defendant who is facing an absolute liability charge may examine his or her *actus reus* for evidence of an involuntary act. A driver cited for speeding may argue that his or her car has defective equipment (speed gauge), which lead to the involuntary act of speeding.

§ 15.10 Requirements for criminal liability in general and for offenses of strict liability and mental culpability.

The minimal requirement for criminal liability is the performance by a person of conduct which includes a voluntary act or the omission to perform an act which he is physically capable of performing. If such conduct is all that is required for commission of a particular offense, or if an offense or some material element thereof does not require a culpable mental state on the part of the actor, such offense is one of "strict liability." If a culpable mental state on the part of the actor is required with respect to every material element of an offense, such offense is one of "mental culpability."

IV. Vicarious Liability

Comment: Vicarious liability does away with the requirement of *actus reus*. Instead of requiring an act by the defendant, an act of another is substituted.

§ 20.00 Criminal liability for conduct of another.

When one person engages in conduct which constitutes an offense, another person is criminally liable for such conduct when, acting with the mental culpability required for the commission thereof, he solicits, requests, commands, importunes, or intentionally aids such person to engage in such conduct.

§ 20.25 Criminal liability of an individual for corporate conduct.

A person is criminally liable for conduct constituting an offense which he performs or causes to be performed in the name of or in behalf of a corporation to the same extent as if such conduct were performed in his own name or behalf.

V. Enterprise Liability

Comment: New York has embraced the idea that a corporation should be held to answer for the acts of high managerial employees. These employees must be acting within the scope of their employment and on behalf of the corporation.

§ 20.20 Criminal liability of corporations.

1. As used in this section:

(a) "Agent" means any director, officer or employee of a corporation, or any other person who is authorized to act in behalf of the corporation.

(b) "High managerial agent" means an officer of a corporation or any other agent in a position of comparable authority with respect to the formulation of corporate policy or the supervision in a managerial capacity of subordinate employees.

2. A corporation is guilty of an offense when:

(a) The conduct constituting the offense consists of an omission to discharge a specific duty of affirmative performance imposed on corporations by law; or

(b) The conduct constituting the offense is engaged in, authorized, solicited, requested, commanded, or recklessly tolerated by the board of directors or by a high managerial agent acting within the scope of his employment and in behalf of the corporation; or

(c) The conduct constituting the offense is engaged in by an agent of the corporation while acting within the scope of his employment and in behalf of the corporation, and the offense is (i) a misdemeanor or a violation, (ii) one defined by a statute which clearly indicates a legislative intent to impose such criminal liability on a corporation, or (iii) any offense set forth in title twenty-seven of article seventy-one of the environmental conservation law.

Questions

1. The XYZ Corporation is paying $10,000 each month to dispose of low-level toxic waste. The board of directors is concerned about this expense and asks the company president if there is any way to lower the cost. The president passes their question down the line. A shift supervisor misinterprets the concern and orders workers to dump the waste into nearby storm drains to save on disposal fees. The toxic waste contaminates the ground water, and tests trace the substance back to the corporation. The dumping of the waste is a violation of the state Environmental Protection Act. Can the corporation be charged with a crime? Can any of the employees be prosecuted for the dumping?

2. Tom's neighbor Mary is mentally challenged. He talks to her for over a month and explains how he wants her to go into a bank and withdraw some money. He tells her to fill out the bank withdrawal slip with the words "I have a gun. Give me all the money." Mary does not fully understand what Tom is asking her to do. She is arrested outside the bank after "withdrawing" some money. Under the statutes in this chapter, can Tom be charged with bank robbery?

Chapter 3
Anticipatory Offenses and Parties to Crimes

I. Solicitation

***Comment*:** Under New York's solicitation statutes, the offender must solicit, request, command, or encourage another person to commit a crime. The offender must also intend that the other person commit the crime. Solicitation is divided into five different degrees. The degree of violation and the class of felony or misdemeanor depends on the crime solicited and, in some cases, the age of the people involved. All five solicitation statutes are similar. The only differences of the statutes are in degrees and class of felony or misdemeanor. The following criminal solicitation statutes, § 100.00–100.13, are a basic description of the contents of the actual statutes.

§ 100.00–100.13 Criminal solicitation (First, Second, Third, Fourth, and Fifth degrees)

A person is guilty of criminal solicitation in the _____ degree when, with intent that another person engage in conduct constituting a class ____ felony/misdemeanor, he solicits, requests, commands, importunes or otherwise attempts to cause such other person to engage in such conduct.

Criminal solicitation in the _______ degree is a class_______ felony/misdemeanor.

§ 100.15 Criminal solicitation; no defense.

It is no defense to a prosecution for criminal solicitation that the person solicited could not be guilty of the crime solicited owing to criminal irresponsibility or other legal incapacity or exemption, or to unawareness of the criminal nature of the conduct solicited or of the defendant's criminal purpose or to other factors precluding the mental state required for the commission of the crime in question.

§ 100.20 Criminal solicitation; exemption.

A person is not guilty of criminal solicitation when his solicitation constitutes conduct of a kind that is necessarily incidental to the commission of the crime solicited. When under such circumstances the solicitation constitutes an offense other than criminal solicitation which is related to but separate from the crime solicited, the actor is guilty of such related and separate offense only and not of criminal solicitation.

II. Attempt

***Comment*:** An offender must have the specific intent to commit the crime he or she attempts. One cannot act with a negligent or reckless state of mind and be convicted of an attempt crime. Also required is an act by the offender that advances toward the completion of the crime. Mere preparation is usually not enough.

§ 110.00 Attempt to commit a crime.

A person is guilty of an attempt to commit a crime when, with intent to commit a crime, he engages in conduct which tends to effect the commission of such crime.

§ 110.05 Attempt to commit a crime; punishment.

An attempt to commit a crime is a:

1. Class A-I felony when the crime attempted is the A-I felony of murder in the first degree, criminal possession of a controlled substance in the first degree, criminal sale of a controlled substance in the first degree, criminal possession of a chemical or biological weapon in the first degree or criminal use of a chemical or biological weapon in the first degree;
2. Class A-II felony when the crime attempted is a class A-II felony;
3. Class B felony when the crime attempted is a class A-I felony except as provided in subdivision one hereof;
4. Class C felony when the crime attempted is a class B felony;
5. Class D felony when the crime attempted is a class C felony;
6. Class E felony when the crime attempted is a class D felony;
7. Class A misdemeanor when the crime attempted is a class E felony;
8. Class B misdemeanor when the crime attempted is a misdemeanor.

§ 110.10 Attempt to commit a crime; no defense.

If the conduct in which a person engages otherwise constitutes an attempt to commit a crime pursuant to section 110.00, it is no defense to a prosecution for such attempt that the crime charged to have been attempted was, under the attendant circumstances, factually or legally impossible of commission, if such crime could have been committed had the attendant circumstances been as such person believed them to be.

III. Conspiracy

***Comment*:** In a criminal conspiracy, two or more people have the intent to commit an offense and agree with each other to commit it. Conspiracy is divided into six different degrees. The degree of violation and the class of felony or misdemeanor depends on the crime that is the object of the agreement and, in some cases, the age of the people involved. All six conspiracy statutes are similar. The only differences within the statutes are in the degrees and class of felony or misdemeanor. The following conspiracy statutes, § 105.00–105.17, are a basic description of the contents of the actual statutes.

§ 105.00–105.17 Conspiracy (First, Second, Third, Fourth, Fifth, and Sixth degrees)

A person is guilty of conspiracy in the _______ degree when, with intent that conduct constituting a class _____ felony/misdemeanor be performed, he being over eighteen years of age, agrees with one or more persons . . . to engage in or cause the performance of such conduct.

Conspiracy in the first degree is a class ____ felony/misdemeanor.

§ 105.20 Conspiracy; pleading and proof; necessity of overt act.

A person shall not be convicted of conspiracy unless an overt act is alleged and proved to have been committed by one of the conspirators in furtherance of the conspiracy.

§ 105.30 Conspiracy; no defense.

It is no defense to a prosecution for conspiracy that, owing to criminal irresponsibility or other legal incapacity or exemption, or to unawareness of the criminal nature of the agreement or the object conduct or of the defendant's criminal purpose or to other factors precluding the mental state required for the commission of conspiracy or the object crime, one or more of the defendant's co-conspirators could not be guilty of conspiracy or the object crime.

IV. Facilitation

***Comment*:** The crime of criminal facilitation occurs when one renders aid to a person who intends to engage in conduct that would constitute a crime. Facilitation is divided into four different degrees. The degree of violation and the class of felony or misdemeanor depends on the crime that is the object of the agreement and, in some cases, the age of the people involved. All four facilitation statutes are similar. The only differences within the statutes are in the degrees and class of felony or misdemeanor. The following criminal facilitation statutes, § 115.00–115.08, are a basic description of the contents of the actual statutes.

§ 115.00–115.08 Criminal facilitation (First, Second, Third, and Fourth degrees)

A person is guilty of criminal facilitation in the ______ degree when, believing it probable that he is rendering aid to a person who intends to commit a class ______ felony/misdemeanor, he engages in conduct which provides such person with means or opportunity for the commission thereof and which in fact aids such person to commit such class ____ felony/misdemeanor.

§ 115.10 Criminal facilitation; no defense.

It is no defense to a prosecution for criminal facilitation that:

1. The person facilitated was not guilty of the underlying felony owing to criminal irresponsibility or other legal incapacity or exemption, or to unawareness of the criminal nature of the conduct in question or to other factors precluding the mental state required for the commission of such felony; or

2. The person facilitated has not been prosecuted for or convicted of the underlying felony, or has previously been acquitted thereof; or

3. The defendant himself is not guilty of the felony which he facilitated because he did not act with the intent or other culpable mental state required for the commission thereof.

§ 115.15 Criminal facilitation; corroboration.

A person shall not be convicted of criminal facilitation upon the testimony of a person who has committed the felony charged to have been facilitated unless such testimony be corroborated by such other evidence as tends to connect the defendant with such facilitation.

__Questions__

1. Mike approaches a woman who is standing on a street corner near a drug house. He asks her to go down the street and buy him drugs, but the woman turns out to be an undercover police officer. Under what statute will Mike be charged?

2. One afternoon, Amanda, Kim, and Ashley meet in a café to discuss robbing a bank. They decide that Amanda will drive the get-a-way car; Ashley, who once worked at the bank, will provide the layout of the bank and the security passwords; and Kim will enter the bank and steal the money. After weeks of discussing and planning, the three women decide not to commit the crime when Ashley fails to obtain the passwords. What statutes in this chapter, if any, apply to this incident?

3. Bob walks into a bank and pulls a gun out of his pocket. Just before he opens his mouth to yell "this is a hold-up," a police car pulls up outside. Bob returns the gun to his pocket and quickly leaves the bank. A customer in the bank observed Bob's actions and he tells the police officer. Bob is arrested a few blocks away. Has Bob made a substantial step toward the commission of bank robbery that he can be convicted of attempt?

Chapter 4
Defenses to Criminal Culpability: Part I

I. Burden of Proof: Affirmative Defense

***Comment*:** An affirmative defense must be raised by the defendant or it will not be considered. Once raised, the defendant must put forth evidence to support the defense. When enough evidence is entered, the prosecution is required to overcome the defense. To obtain a conviction, the prosecutor must convince a judge or jury that the affirmative defense is not valid using the proof standard of "beyond a reasonable doubt."

§ 25.00 Defenses; burden of proof.

1. When a "defense," other than an "affirmative defense," defined by statute is raised at a trial, the people have the burden of disproving such defense beyond a reasonable doubt.

2. When a defense declared by statute to be an "affirmative defense" is raised at a trial, the defendant has the burden of establishing such defense by a preponderance of the evidence.

II. Ignorance or Mistake

***Comment*:** *Mistake of fact* is not a defense in the state of New York, except for a few exceptions reserved by section 15.20 listed below. Mistake or ignorance of a fact is only a defense if it negates the mental state required by a statute or if it is allowed by another statute.

Mistake or ignorance of a law is never a defense, unless the defendant relied on an official statement of the law. Our society has a great many laws—so many laws that even veteran lawyers and judges do not know them all. However, our legal system works on the assumption that everyone "knows" every law. The alternative of allowing an "ignorance of the law" defense would result in few convictions.

§ 15.20 Effect of ignorance or mistake upon liability.

1. A person is not relieved of criminal liability for conduct because he engages in such conduct under a mistaken belief of fact, unless:

(a) Such factual mistake negatives the culpable mental state required for the commission of an offense; or

(b) The statute defining the offense or a statute related thereto expressly provides that such factual mistake constitutes a defense or exemption; or

(c) Such factual mistake is of a kind that supports a defense of justification as defined in article thirty-five of this chapter.

2. A person is not relieved of criminal liability for conduct because he engages in such conduct under a mistaken belief that it does not, as a matter of law, constitute an offense, unless such mistaken belief is founded upon an official statement of the law contained in (a) a statute or other

enactment, or (b) an administrative order or grant of permission, or (c) a judicial decision of a state or federal court, or (d) an interpretation of the statute or law relating to the offense, officially made or issued by a public servant, agency or body legally charged or empowered with the responsibility or privilege of administering, enforcing or interpreting such statute or law.

3. Notwithstanding the use of the term "knowingly" in any provision of this chapter defining an offense in which the age of a child is an element thereof, knowledge by the defendant of the age of such child is not an element of any such offense and it is not, unless expressly so provided, a defense to a prosecution therefor that the defendant did not know the age of the child or believed such age to be the same as or greater than that specified in the statute.

4. Notwithstanding the use of the term "knowingly" in any provision of this chapter defining an offense in which the aggregate weight of a controlled substance or marihuana is an element, knowledge by the defendant of the aggregate weight of such controlled substance or marihuana is not an element of any such offense and it is not, unless expressly so provided, a defense to a prosecution therefor that the defendant did not know the aggregate weight of the controlled substance or marihuana.

III. Compulsion (Duress)

***Comment*:** Except in the case of murder, criminal conduct is excused if that conduct is the result of a threat of great bodily harm or death. This threat must be reasonable and imminent.

§ 40.00 Duress.

1. In any prosecution for an offense, it is an affirmative defense that the defendant engaged in the proscribed conduct because he was coerced to do so by the use or threatened imminent use of unlawful physical force upon him or a third person, which force or threatened force a person of reasonable firmness in his situation would have been unable to resist.

2. The defense of duress as defined in subdivision one of this section is not available when a person intentionally or recklessly places himself in a situation in which it is probable that he will be subjected to duress.

IV. Justification

***Comment*:** Criminal conduct can be excused if that conduct was performed to avoid a greater injury. The offender's situation cannot be of his or her own making.

§ 35.00 Justification; a defense.

In any prosecution for an offense, justification, as defined in sections 35.05 through 35.30, is a defense.

§ 35.05 Justification; generally.

Unless otherwise limited by the ensuing provisions of this article defining justifiable use of physical force, conduct which would otherwise constitute an offense is justifiable and not criminal when:

1. Such conduct is required or authorized by law or by a judicial decree, or is performed by a public servant in the reasonable exercise of his official powers, duties or functions; or

2. Such conduct is necessary as an emergency measure to avoid an imminent public or private injury which is about to occur by reason of a situation occasioned or developed through no fault of the actor, and which is of such gravity that, according to ordinary standards of intelligence and morality, the desirability and urgency of avoiding such injury clearly outweigh the desirability of avoiding the injury sought to be prevented by the statute defining the offense in issue. The necessity and justifiability of such conduct may not rest upon considerations pertaining only to the morality and advisability of the statute, either in its general application or with respect to its application to a particular class of cases arising thereunder. Whenever evidence relating to the defense of justification under this subdivision is offered by the defendant, the court shall rule as a matter of law whether the claimed facts and circumstances would, if established, constitute a defense.

V. Infancy

***Comment*:** Children 16 years of age and under cannot be held criminally responsible for an offense unless the act is one of the crimes listed in subdivision two.

§ 30.00 Infancy.

1. Except as provided in subdivision two of this section, a person less than sixteen years old is not criminally responsible for conduct.

2. A person thirteen, fourteen or fifteen years of age is criminally responsible for acts constituting murder in the second degree as defined in subdivisions one and two of section 125.25 and in subdivision three of such section provided that the underlying crime for the murder charge is one for which such person is criminally responsible; and a person fourteen or fifteen years of age is criminally responsible for acts constituting the crimes defined in section 135.25 (kidnapping in the first degree); 150.20 (arson in the first degree); subdivisions one and two of section 120.10 (assault in the first degree); 125.20 (manslaughter in the first degree); subdivisions one and two of section 130.35 (rape in the first degree); subdivisions one and two of section 130.50 (criminal sexual act in the first degree); 130.70 (aggravated sexual abuse in the first degree); 140.30 (burglary in the first degree); subdivision one of section 140.25 (burglary in the second degree); 150.15 (arson in the second degree); 160.15 (robbery in the first degree); subdivision two of section 160.10 (robbery in the second degree) of this chapter; subdivision four of section 265.02 of this chapter, where such firearm is possessed on school grounds, as that phrase is defined in subdivision fourteen of section 220.00 of this chapter; or section 265.03 of this chapter, where such machine gun or such firearm is possessed on school grounds, as that phrase is defined in subdivision fourteen of section 220.00 of this chapter; or defined in this chapter as an attempt to commit murder in the second degree or kidnapping in the first degree.

3. In any prosecution for an offense, lack of criminal responsibility by reason of infancy, as defined in this section, is a defense.

VI. Insanity

***Comment*:** To determine whether a defendant is insane, New York has adopted the Substantial Capacity Test. To be successful with the defense of insanity, a defendant must show he or she has a mental disease or defect, and that because of that disease or defect he or she lacks substantial capacity to know the nature and consequences of the criminal conduct or that such conduct was wrong.

The defendant has the burden of first bringing up the defense and showing evidence that he or she was legally insane at the time of the offense. Once the defense's evidence has been established, the prosecution will then have to prove beyond a reasonable doubt that the defendant was sane.

Students should understand that most offenders who suffer from mental illness are not usually *legally* insane. A person can suffer from various mental illnesses and still not fit the requirements needed to be considered legally insane.

§ 40.15 Mental disease or defect.

In any prosecution for an offense, it is an affirmative defense that when the defendant engaged in the proscribed conduct, he lacked criminal responsibility by reason of mental disease or defect.

Such lack of criminal responsibility means that at the time of such conduct, as a result of mental disease or defect, he lacked substantial capacity to know or appreciate either:

1. The nature and consequences of such conduct; or

2. That such conduct was wrong.

VII. Entrapment

***Comment*:** The key to understanding entrapment is to examine whether or not the defendant was predisposed to commit the offense. For the defense of entrapment to work, a government agent must have incited or induced the defendant, who had no interest in committing the offense.

§ 40.05 Entrapment.

In any prosecution for an offense, it is an affirmative defense that the defendant engaged in the proscribed conduct because he was induced or encouraged to do so by a public servant, or by a person acting in cooperation with a public servant, seeking to obtain evidence against him for purpose of criminal prosecution, and when the methods used to obtain such evidence were such as to create a substantial risk that the offense would be committed by a person not otherwise disposed to commit it. Inducement or encouragement to commit an offense means active inducement or encouragement. Conduct merely affording a person an opportunity to commit an offense does not constitute entrapment.

VIII. Use of Force (Self-defense of Persons and Property)

Comment: New York law allows one to legally employ self-defense if one has a reasonable belief that unlawful force is about to be used against him or her. The person claiming the defense cannot be the aggressor, and the amount of force must be reasonable under the circumstances and must end when the threat ends. If a person is under attack, a bystander may defend him or her with the same level of force the victim is entitled to use.

Deadly force can be used when it is reasonably believed that such force is required to prevent imminent death or great bodily harm. Before using deadly force, there is a duty to retreat unless one of the listed circumstances is present.

Reasonable nondeadly force may be used to prevent an entry into a dwelling or the simple trespass of a real or personal property. One of the main issues in self-defense actions is to know when an individual's rights cease. In any self-defense action, the right to use force ends once the threat stops. A victim cannot track the suspect down the next day and employ his or her right of "self defense."

§ 35.10 Justification; use of physical force generally.

The use of physical force upon another person which would otherwise constitute an offense is justifiable and not criminal under any of the following circumstances:

1. A parent, guardian or other person entrusted with the care and supervision of a person under the age of twenty-one or an incompetent person, and a teacher or other person entrusted with the care and supervision of a person under the age of twenty-one for a special purpose, may use physical force, but not deadly physical force, upon such person when and to the extent that he reasonably believes it necessary to maintain discipline or to promote the welfare of such person.

2. A warden or other authorized official of a jail, prison or correctional institution may, in order to maintain order and discipline, use such physical force as is authorized by the correction law.

3. A person responsible for the maintenance of order in a common carrier of passengers, or a person acting under his direction, may use physical force when and to the extent that he reasonably believes it necessary to maintain order, but he may use deadly physical force only when he reasonably believes it necessary to prevent death or serious physical injury.

4. A person acting under a reasonable belief that another person is about to commit suicide or to inflict serious physical injury upon himself may use physical force upon such person to the extent that he reasonably believes it necessary to thwart such result.

5. A duly licensed physician, or a person acting under a physician's direction, may use physical force for the purpose of administering a recognized form of treatment which he or she reasonably believes to be adapted to promoting the physical or mental health of the patient if (a) the treatment is administered with the consent of the patient or, if the patient is under the age of eighteen years or an incompetent person, with the consent of the parent, guardian or other person entrusted with the patient's care and supervision, or (b) the treatment is administered in an emergency when the physician reasonably believes that no one competent to consent can be consulted and that a reasonable person, wishing to safeguard the welfare of the patient, would consent.

6. A person may, pursuant to the ensuing provisions of this article, use physical force upon another person in self-defense or defense of a third person, or in defense of premises, or in order to prevent larceny of or criminal mischief to property, or in order to effect an arrest or prevent an escape from custody. Whenever a person is authorized by any such provision to use deadly physical force in any given circumstance, nothing contained in any other such provision may be deemed to negate or qualify such authorization.

§ 35.15 Justification; use of physical force in defense of a person.

1. A person may, subject to the provisions of subdivision two, use physical force upon another person when and to the extent he or she reasonably believes such to be necessary to defend himself, herself or a third person from what he or she reasonably believes to be the use or imminent use of unlawful physical force by such other person, unless:

(a) The latter's conduct was provoked by the actor with intent to cause physical injury to another person; or

(b) The actor was the initial aggressor; except that in such case the use of physical force is nevertheless justifiable if the actor has withdrawn from the encounter and effectively communicated such withdrawal to such other person but the latter persists in continuing the incident by the use or threatened imminent use of unlawful physical force; or

(c) The physical force involved is the product of a combat by agreement not specifically authorized by law.

2. A person may not use deadly physical force upon another person under circumstances specified in subdivision one unless:

(a) The actor reasonably believes that such other person is using or about to use deadly physical force. Even in such case, however, the actor may not use deadly physical force if he or she knows that with complete personal safety, to oneself and others he or she may avoid the necessity of so doing by retreating; except that the actor is under no duty to retreat if he or she is:

(i) in his or her dwelling and not the initial aggressor; or

(ii) a police officer or peace officer or a person assisting a police officer or a peace officer at the latter's direction, acting pursuant to section 35.30; or

(b) He or she reasonably believes that such other person is committing or attempting to commit a kidnapping, forcible rape, forcible criminal sexual act or robbery; or

(c) He or she reasonably believes that such other person is committing or attempting to commit a burglary, and the circumstances are such that the use of deadly physical force is authorized by subdivision three of section 35.20.

§ 35.20 Justification; use of physical force in defense of premises and in defense of a person in the course of burglary.

1. Any person may use physical force upon another person when he or she reasonably believes such to be necessary to prevent or terminate what he or she reasonably believes to be the commission or attempted commission by such other person of a crime involving damage to

premises. Such person may use any degree of physical force, other than deadly physical force, which he or she reasonably believes to be necessary for such purpose, and may use deadly physical force if he or she reasonably believes such to be necessary to prevent or terminate the commission or attempted commission of arson.

2. A person in possession or control of any premises, or a person licensed or privileged to be thereon or therein, may use physical force upon another person when he or she reasonably believes such to be necessary to prevent or terminate what he or she reasonably believes to be the commission or attempted commission by such other person of a criminal trespass upon such premises. Such person may use any degree of physical force, other than deadly physical force, which he or she reasonably believes to be necessary for such purpose, and may use deadly physical force in order to prevent or terminate the commission or attempted commission of arson, as prescribed in subdivision one, or in the course of a burglary or attempted burglary, as prescribed in subdivision three.

3. A person in possession or control of, or licensed or privileged to be in, a dwelling or an occupied building, who reasonably believes that another person is committing or attempting to commit a burglary of such dwelling or building, may use deadly physical force upon such other person when he or she reasonably believes such to be necessary to prevent or terminate the commission or attempted commission of such burglary.

4. As used in this section, the following terms have the following meanings:

(a) The terms "premises," "building" and "dwelling" have the meanings prescribed in section 140.00;

(b) Persons "licensed or privileged" to be in buildings or upon other premises include, but are not limited to:

(i) police officers or peace officers acting in the performance of their duties; and

(ii) security personnel or employees of nuclear powered electric generating facilities located within the state who are employed as part of any security plan approved by the federal operating license agencies acting in the performance of their duties at such generating facilities. For purposes of this subparagraph, the term "nuclear powered electric generating facility" shall mean a facility that generates electricity using nuclear power for sale, directly or indirectly, to the public, including the land upon which the facility is located and the safety and security zones as defined under federal regulations.

§ 35.25 Justification; use of physical force to prevent or terminate larceny or criminal mischief.

A person may use physical force, other than deadly physical force, upon another person when and to the extent that he or she reasonably believes such to be necessary to prevent or terminate what he or she reasonably believes to be the commission or attempted commission by such other person of larceny or of criminal mischief with respect to property other than premises.

IX. Use of Force to Make an Arrest

***Comment*:** Law enforcement officers and private citizens who enforce the law are allowed to use reasonable force to make an arrest. There is no requirement to retreat before force is used.

Deadly force can only be used when it is reasonably believed that such force is required to prevent imminent death or great bodily harm. The deadly force option for police officers is expanded beyond that of the private citizen to include the ability to stop a fleeing suspect. When used to stop a fleeing suspect, it must be reasonably believed that (1) it is needed to prevent escape and (2) the suspect is capable of committing great bodily harm or murdering the officer or another person unless he or she is arrested immediately. Factors to consider include whether a deadly weapon is being used to aid in the escape and statements or facts indicating that the felon is an imminent danger to human life or has the ability to inflict great bodily harm unless he or she is immediately arrested. This statute is in line with the holding of the case *Tennessee v. Garner* discussed in the text.

§ 35.27 Justification; use of physical force in resisting arrest prohibited.

A person may not use physical force to resist an arrest, whether authorized or unauthorized, which is being effected or attempted by a police officer or peace officer when it would reasonably appear that the latter is a police officer or peace officer.

§ 35.30 Justification; use of physical force in making an arrest or in preventing an escape.

1. A police officer or a peace officer, in the course of effecting or attempting to effect an arrest, or of preventing or attempting to prevent the escape from custody, of a person whom he or she reasonably believes to have committed an offense, may use physical force when and to the extent he or she reasonably believes such to be necessary to effect the arrest, or to prevent the escape from custody, or in self-defense or to defend a third person from what he or she reasonably believes to be the use or imminent use of physical force; except that deadly physical force may be used for such purposes only when he or she reasonably believes that:

(a) The offense committed by such person was:

(i) a felony or an attempt to commit a felony involving the use or attempted use or threatened imminent use of physical force against a person; or

(ii) kidnapping, arson, escape in the first degree, burglary in the first degree or any attempt to commit such a crime; or

(b) The offense committed or attempted by such person was a felony and that, in the course of resisting arrest therefor or attempting to escape from custody, such person is armed with a firearm or deadly weapon; or

(c) Regardless of the particular offense which is the subject of the arrest or attempted escape, the use of deadly physical force is necessary to defend the police officer or peace officer or another person from what the officer reasonably believes to be the use or imminent use of deadly physical force.

2. The fact that a police officer or a peace officer is justified in using deadly physical force under circumstances prescribed in paragraphs (a) and (b) of subdivision one does not constitute justification for reckless conduct by such police officer or peace officer amounting to an offense against or with respect to innocent persons whom he or she is not seeking to arrest or retain in custody.

3. A person who has been directed by a police officer or a peace officer to assist such police officer or peace officer to effect an arrest or to prevent an escape from custody may use physical force, other than deadly physical force, when and to the extent that he or she reasonably believes such to be necessary to carry out such police officer's or peace officer's direction, unless he or she knows that the arrest or prospective arrest is not or was not authorized and may use deadly physical force under such circumstances when:

(a) He or she reasonably believes such to be necessary for self-defense or to defend a third person from what he or she reasonably believes to be the use or imminent use of deadly physical force; or

(b) He or she is directed or authorized by such police officer or peace officer to use deadly physical force unless he or she knows that the police officer or peace officer is not authorized to use deadly physical force under the circumstances.

4. A private person acting on his or her own account may use physical force, other than deadly physical force, upon another person when and to the extent that he or she reasonably believes such to be necessary to effect an arrest or to prevent the escape from custody of a person whom he or she reasonably believes to have committed an offense and who in fact has committed such offense; and may use deadly physical force for such purpose when he or she reasonably believes such to be necessary to:

(a) Defend himself, herself or a third person from what he or she reasonably believes to be the use or imminent use of deadly physical force; or

(b) Effect the arrest of a person who has committed murder, manslaughter in the first degree, robbery, forcible rape or forcible criminal sexual act and who is in immediate flight therefrom.

5. A guard, police officer or peace officer who is charged with the duty of guarding prisoners in a detention facility, as that term is defined in section 205.00, or while in transit to or from a detention facility, may use physical force when and to the extent that he or she reasonably believes such to be necessary to prevent the escape of a prisoner from a detention facility or from custody while in transit thereto or therefrom.

Questions

1. Mike arrives home just as Frank runs out of his door carrying Mike's DVD player. Frank runs down the block and Mike follows him in his car. Mike decides that the only way to get his player back is to run over Frank, who suffers serious injuries from the attack. Does Mike have a valid defense?

2. Jill holds Hank at gunpoint and locks a bomb around his neck. She tells him he must rob a nearby bank or the bomb will be set off. He robs the bank and gives the money to Jill before she releases him. Hank is arrested for bank robbery. Does he have a valid defense?

3. Tom is driving through a snowstorm. As the storm turns into a blizzard, his car runs out of gas in front of the only house for miles around. He knocks on the door but no one is home. Tom breaks into the home to avoid freezing. Does he have a valid defense?

4. Two teenage kids drive by Ted's mailbox and smash it with a baseball bat. As they drive off down the road, Ted, who is on his front porch, fires a shot from his rifle and kills the passenger. Ted claims self-defense because the kid had a bat. Under the statutes in this chapter, will his defense work?

5. Someone has kidnapped your children and threatens to harm them unless you commit a bank robbery. If prosecuted for the bank robbery, will you have a defense?

6. An 18-year-old drug dealer wants a rival dead. He gives a handgun to a 7-year-old boy and tells the child to point the gun at the rival and pull the trigger as many times as he can. The boy does what he is told and the rival dies from the gunshot wounds. Under the statutes in this chapter, does the child have a defense?

9. Hank pulls a knife out of his pocket, threatens to kill Bob, and begins to move toward him. Bob smashes a chair across Hank's head killing him. Under the statutes in this chapter, what defense, if any, applies?

10. The police place a brand new color TV in the back of a pickup truck and park it in the parking lot of a local bar. The police then take up positions to watch the truck. Two drunks come out of the bar and see the TV. They take it and put it into their own car and attempt to leave the lot. The police arrest them for theft. Under the statutes in this chapter, do the two men have a defense?

11. Under the statutes in this chapter, how much force can a person use when he or she is threatened with immediate physical harm?

Chapter 5
Defenses to Criminal Culpability: Part II

I. Intoxication

***Comment*:** In the following statute, New York makes intoxicated people responsible for their own actions. While rarely successful, the statute does allow a defendant to argue that his or her intoxication negated an element of the crime they are being charged for.

§ 15.25 Effect of intoxication upon liability.

Intoxication is not, as such, a defense to a criminal charge; but in any prosecution for an offense, evidence of intoxication of the defendant may be offered by the defendant whenever it is relevant to negative an element of the crime charged.

II. Consent (Sex Crime)

***Comment*:** Consent to engage in sexual conduct, in regards to sex crimes, is codified in the statutes that follow. Instead of defining what consent is, statute 130.05 defines the "lack of consent." The following statutes also list persons who are deemed incapable of consenting to sex. Initial consent to sex can be withdrawn. If consent is removed, a defense is not available for forced sexual activity.

§ 130.05 Sex offenses; lack of consent.

1. Whether or not specifically stated, it is an element of every offense defined in this article that the sexual act was committed without consent of the victim.

2. Lack of consent results from:

(a) Forcible compulsion; or

(b) Incapacity to consent; or

(c) Where the offense charged is sexual abuse or forcible touching, any circumstances, in addition to forcible compulsion or incapacity to consent, in which the victim does not expressly or impliedly acquiesce in the actor's conduct; or

(d) Where the offense charged is rape in the third degree as defined in subdivision three of section 130.25, or criminal sexual act in the third degree as defined in subdivision three of section 130.40, in addition to forcible compulsion, circumstances under which, at the time of the act of intercourse, oral sexual conduct or anal sexual conduct, the victim clearly expressed that he or she did not consent to engage in such act, and a reasonable person in the actor's situation would have understood such person's words and acts as an expression of lack of consent to such act under all the circumstances.

3. A person is deemed incapable of consent when he or she is:

(a) less than seventeen years old; or

(b) mentally disabled; or

(c) mentally incapacitated; or

(d) physically helpless; or

(e) committed to the care and custody of the state department of correctional services or a hospital, as such term is defined in subdivision two of section four hundred of the correction law, and the actor is an employee, not married to such person, who knows or reasonably should know that such person is committed to the care and custody of such department or hospital. For purposes of this paragraph, "employee" means (i) an employee of the state department of correctional services who performs professional duties in a state correctional facility consisting of providing custody, medical or mental health services, counseling services, educational programs, or vocational training for inmates;

(ii) an employee of the division of parole who performs professional duties in a state correctional facility and who provides institutional parole services pursuant to section two hundred fifty-nine-e of the executive law; or

(iii) an employee of the office of mental health who performs professional duties in a state correctional facility or hospital, as such term is defined in subdivision two of section four hundred of the correction law, consisting of providing custody, or medical or mental health services for such inmates; or

(f) committed to the care and custody of a local correctional facility, as such term is defined in subdivision two of section forty of the correction law, and the actor is an employee, not married to such person, who knows or reasonably should know that such person is committed to the care and custody of such facility. For purposes of this paragraph, "employee" means an employee of the local correctional facility where the person is committed who performs professional duties consisting of providing custody, medical or mental health services, counseling services, educational services, or vocational training for inmates; or

(g) committed to or placed with the office of children and family services and in residential care, and the actor is an employee, not married to such person, who knows or reasonably should know that such person is committed to or placed with such office of children and family services and in residential care. For purposes of this paragraph, "employee" means an employee of the office of children and family services or of a residential facility who performs duties consisting of providing custody, medical or mental health services, counseling services, educational services, or vocational training for persons committed to or placed with the office of children and family services and in residential care; or

(h) a client or patient and the actor is a health care provider or mental health care provider charged with rape in the third degree as defined in section 130.25, criminal sexual act in the third degree as defined in section 130.40, aggravated sexual abuse in the fourth degree as defined in section 130.65-a, or sexual abuse in the third degree as defined in section 130.55, and the act of sexual conduct occurs during a treatment session, consultation, interview, or examination.

§ 130.10 Sex offenses; limitation; defenses.

1. In any prosecution under this article in which the victim's lack of consent is based solely upon his or her incapacity to consent because he or she was mentally disabled, mentally incapacitated

or physically helpless, it is an affirmative defense that the defendant, at the time he or she engaged in the conduct constituting the offense, did not know of the facts or conditions responsible for such incapacity to consent.

2. Conduct performed for a valid medical or mental health care purpose shall not constitute a violation of any section of this article in which incapacity to consent is based on the circumstances set forth in paragraph (h) of subdivision three of section 130.05 of this article.

3. In any prosecution for the crime of rape in the third degree as defined in section 130.25, criminal sexual act in the third degree as defined in section 130.40, aggravated sexual abuse in the fourth degree as defined in section 130.65-a, or sexual abuse in the third degree as defined in section 130.55 in which incapacity to consent is based on the circumstances set forth in paragraph (h) of subdivision three of section 130. 05 of this article it shall be an affirmative defense that the client or patient consented to such conduct charged after having been expressly advised by the health care or mental health care provider that such conduct was not performed for a valid medical purpose.

4. In any prosecution under this article in which the victim's lack of consent is based solely on his or her incapacity to consent because he or she was less than seventeen years old, mentally disabled, or a client or patient and the actor is a health care provider, it shall be a defense that the defendant was married to the victim as defined in subdivision four of section 130.00 of this article.

Questions

1. Julie is out on her first date with Jim, who has taken her to a nice restaurant in town. When Julie excuses herself to go to the ladies room, Jim slips a drug into her tea. Julie returns and finishes her meal and her tea. On their way home, Julie passes out and Jim has sexual intercourse with her. Based on the statutes in this chapter, can Jim argue that Julie consented to sex?

2. Helen and Ted have been drinking. Both of them consent to sex, but during the act Helen becomes unconscious because of her heavy drinking. Ted continues with the sex act. According to the statutes in this chapter, is the defense of consent available to Ted?

3. One night Todd is drinking and using drugs. He returns to his apartment and discovers his key doesn't work. He forces the door open and falls asleep on the sofa. Unknown to him, he has broken into his neighbor's apartment. He is arrested and charged with criminal trespass. Does Todd have a defense?

Chapter 6
Criminal Homicide

Comment: New York follows many other states by classifying homicide into first-degree and second-degree murder and various types of negligent homicide and manslaughter.

§ 125.00 Homicide defined.

Homicide means conduct which causes the death of a person or an unborn child with which a female has been pregnant for more than twenty-four weeks under circumstances constituting murder, manslaughter in the first degree, manslaughter in the second degree, criminally negligent homicide, abortion in the first degree or self-abortion in the first degree.

I. First-degree Murder

Comment: A homicide that is considered first-degree murder requires an intent to kill and the presence of special circumstances that the legislature have deemed worthy of the death sentence. These circumstances include contract killing or the killing of a police officer or a correctional officer.

§ 125.27 Murder in the first degree.

A person is guilty of murder in the first degree when:

1. With intent to cause the death of another person, he causes the death of such person or of a third person; and

(a) Either:

(i) the intended victim was a police officer as defined in subdivision 34 of section 1.20 of the criminal procedure law who was at the time of the killing engaged in the course of performing his official duties, and the defendant knew or reasonably should have known that the intended victim was a police officer; or

(ii) the intended victim was a peace officer as defined in paragraph a of subdivision twenty-one, subdivision twenty-three, twenty-four or sixty-two (employees of the division for youth) of section 2.10 of the criminal procedure law who was at the time of the killing engaged in the course of performing his official duties, and the defendant knew or reasonably should have known that the intended victim was such a uniformed court officer, parole officer, probation officer, or employee of the division for youth; or

(iii) the intended victim was an employee of a state correctional institution or was an employee of a local correctional facility as defined in subdivision two of section forty of the correction law, who was at the time of the killing engaged in the course of performing his official duties, and the defendant knew or reasonably should have known that the intended victim was an employee of a state correctional institution or a local correctional facility; or

(iv) at the time of the commission of the killing, the defendant was confined in a state correctional institution or was otherwise in custody upon a sentence for the term of his natural life, or upon a sentence commuted to one of natural life, or upon a sentence for an indeterminate term the minimum of which was at least fifteen years and the maximum of which was natural life, or at the time of the commission of the killing, the defendant had escaped from such confinement or custody while serving such a sentence and had not yet been returned to such confinement or custody; or

(v) the intended victim was a witness to a crime committed on a prior occasion and the death was caused for the purpose of preventing the intended victim's testimony in any criminal action or proceeding whether or not such action or proceeding had been commenced, or the intended victim had previously testified in a criminal action or proceeding and the killing was committed for the purpose of exacting retribution for such prior testimony, or the intended victim was an immediate family member of a witness to a crime committed on a prior occasion and the killing was committed for the purpose of preventing or influencing the testimony of such witness, or the intended victim was an immediate family member of a witness who had previously testified in a criminal action or proceeding and the killing was committed for the purpose of exacting retribution upon such witness for such prior testimony. As used in this subparagraph "immediate family member" means a husband, wife, father, mother, daughter, son, brother, sister, stepparent, grandparent, stepchild or grandchild; or

(vi) the defendant committed the killing or procured commission of the killing pursuant to an agreement with a person other than the intended victim to commit the same for the receipt, or in expectation of the receipt, of anything of pecuniary value from a party to the agreement or from a person other than the intended victim acting at the direction of a party to such agreement; or

(vii) the victim was killed while the defendant was in the course of committing or attempting to commit and in furtherance of robbery, burglary in the first degree or second degree, kidnapping in the first degree, arson in the first degree or second degree, rape in the first degree, criminal sexual act in the first degree, sexual abuse in the first degree, aggravated sexual abuse in the first degree or escape in the first degree, or in the course of and furtherance of immediate flight after committing or attempting to commit any such crime or in the course of and furtherance of immediate flight after attempting to commit the crime of murder in the second degree; provided however, the victim is not a participant in one of the aforementioned crimes and, provided further that, unless the defendant's criminal liability under this subparagraph is based upon the defendant having commanded another person to cause the death of the victim or intended victim pursuant to section 20.00 of this chapter, this subparagraph shall not apply where the defendant's criminal liability is based upon the conduct of another pursuant to section 20.00 of this chapter; or

(viii) as part of the same criminal transaction, the defendant, with intent to cause serious physical injury to or the death of an additional person or persons, causes the death of an additional person or persons; provided, however, the victim is not a participant in the criminal transaction; or

(ix) prior to committing the killing, the defendant had been convicted of murder as defined in this section or section 125.25 of this article, or had been convicted in another jurisdiction of an offense which, if committed in this state, would constitute a violation of either of such sections; or

(x) the defendant acted in an especially cruel and wanton manner pursuant to a course of conduct intended to inflict and inflicting torture upon the victim prior to the victim's death. As used in this subparagraph, "torture" means the intentional and depraved infliction of extreme physical pain; "depraved" means the defendant relished the infliction of extreme physical pain upon the victim evidencing debasement or perversion or that the defendant evidenced a sense of pleasure in the infliction of extreme physical pain; or

(xi) the defendant intentionally caused the death of two or more additional persons within the state in separate criminal transactions within a period of twenty-four months when committed in a similar fashion or pursuant to a common scheme or plan; or

(xii) the intended victim was a judge as defined in subdivision twenty-three of section 1.20 of the criminal procedure law and the defendant killed such victim because such victim was, at the time of the killing, a judge; or

(xiii) the victim was killed in furtherance of an act of terrorism, as defined in paragraph (b) of subdivision one of section 490.05 of this chapter; and

(b) The defendant was more than eighteen years old at the time of the commission of the crime.

2. In any prosecution under subdivision one, it is an affirmative defense that:

(a) The defendant acted under the influence of extreme emotional disturbance for which there was a reasonable explanation or excuse, the reasonableness of which is to be determined from the viewpoint of a person in the defendant's situation under the circumstances as the defendant believed them to be. Nothing contained in this paragraph shall constitute a defense to a prosecution for, or preclude a conviction of, manslaughter in the first degree or any other crime except murder in the second degree; or

(b) The defendant's conduct consisted of causing or aiding, without the use of duress or deception, another person to commit suicide. Nothing contained in this paragraph shall constitute a defense to a prosecution for, or preclude a conviction of, manslaughter in the second degree or any other crime except murder in the second degree.

Murder in the first degree is a class A-I felony.

II. Second-degree Murder

***Comment*:** The second-degree murder statute uses many of the same elements as the first-degree murder statute. The main differences are the lack of special circumstances and the allowance of affirmative defenses. Deaths resulting from the commission of a dangerous felony (felony murder) are covered under this statute.

§ 125.25 Murder in the second degree.

A person is guilty of murder in the second degree when:

1. With intent to cause the death of another person, he causes the death of such person or of a third person; except that in any prosecution under this subdivision, it is an affirmative defense that:

(a) The defendant acted under the influence of extreme emotional disturbance for which there was a reasonable explanation or excuse, the reasonableness of which is to be determined from the viewpoint of a person in the defendant's situation under the circumstances as the defendant believed them to be. Nothing contained in this paragraph shall constitute a defense to a prosecution for, or preclude a conviction of, manslaughter in the first degree or any other crime; or

(b) The defendant's conduct consisted of causing or aiding, without the use of duress or deception, another person to commit suicide. Nothing contained in this paragraph shall constitute a defense to a prosecution for, or preclude a conviction of, manslaughter in the second degree or any other crime; or

2. Under circumstances evincing a depraved indifference to human life, he recklessly engages in conduct which creates a grave risk of death to another person, and thereby causes the death of another person; or

3. Acting either alone or with one or more other persons, he commits or attempts to commit robbery, burglary, kidnapping, arson, rape in the first degree, criminal sexual act in the first degree, sexual abuse in the first degree, aggravated sexual abuse, escape in the first degree, or escape in the second degree, and, in the course of and in furtherance of such crime or of immediate flight therefrom, he, or another participant, if there be any, causes the death of a person other than one of the participants; except that in any prosecution under this subdivision, in which the defendant was not the only participant in the underlying crime, it is an affirmative defense that the defendant:

(a) Did not commit the homicidal act or in any way solicit, request, command, importune, cause or aid the commission thereof; and

(b) Was not armed with a deadly weapon, or any instrument, article or substance readily capable of causing death or serious physical injury and of a sort not ordinarily carried in public places by law-abiding persons; and

(c) Had no reasonable ground to believe that any other participant was armed with such a weapon, instrument, article or substance; and

(d) Had no reasonable ground to believe that any other participant intended to engage in conduct likely to result in death or serious physical injury; or

4. Under circumstances evincing a depraved indifference to human life, and being eighteen years old or more the defendant recklessly engages in conduct which creates a grave risk of serious physical injury or death to another person less than eleven years old and thereby causes the death of such person; or

5. Being eighteen years old or more, while in the course of committing rape in the first, second or third degree, criminal sexual act in the first, second or third degree, sexual abuse in the first degree, aggravated sexual abuse in the first, second, third or fourth degree, or incest in the first, second or third degree, against a person less than fourteen years old, he or she intentionally causes the death of such person.

Murder in the second degree is a class A-I felony

§ 125.26 Aggravated murder.

A person is guilty of aggravated murder when:

1. With intent to cause the death of another person, he or she causes the death of such person, or of a third person who was a person described in subparagraph (i), (ii) or (iii) of paragraph (a) of this subdivision engaged at the time of the killing in the course of performing his or her official duties; and

(a) Either:

(i) the intended victim was a police officer as defined in subdivision thirty-four of section 1.20 of the criminal procedure law who was at the time of the killing engaged in the course of performing his or her official duties, and the defendant knew or reasonably should have known that the victim was a police officer; or

(ii) the intended victim was a peace officer as defined in paragraph a of subdivision twenty-one, subdivision twenty-three, twenty-four or sixty-two (employees of the division for youth) of section 2.10 of the criminal procedure law who was at the time of the killing engaged in the course of performing his or her official duties, and the defendant knew or reasonably should have known that the victim was such a uniformed court officer, parole officer, probation officer, or employee of the division for youth; or

(iii) the intended victim was an employee of a state correctional institution or was an employee of a local correctional facility as defined in subdivision two of section forty of the correction law, who was at the time of the killing engaged in the course of performing his or her official duties, and the defendant knew or reasonably should have known that the victim was an employee of a state correctional institution or a local correctional facility; and

(b) The defendant was more than eighteen years old at the time of the commission of the crime.

2. In any prosecution under subdivision one of this section, it is an affirmative defense that:

(a) The defendant acted under the influence of extreme emotional disturbance for which there was a reasonable explanation or excuse, the reasonableness of which is to be determined from the viewpoint of a person in the defendant's situation under the circumstances as the defendant believed them to be. Nothing contained in this paragraph shall constitute a defense to a prosecution for, or preclude a conviction of, aggravated manslaughter in the first degree, manslaughter in the first degree or any other crime except murder in the second degree; or

(b) The defendant's conduct consisted of causing or aiding, without the use of duress or deception, another person to commit suicide. Nothing contained in this paragraph shall constitute a defense to a prosecution for, or preclude a conviction of, aggravated manslaughter in the second degree, manslaughter in the second degree or any other crime except murder in the second degree.

Aggravated murder is a class A-I felony.

III. Negligent Homicide

Comment: Under section 15.05 (4) of the Model Penal Code: "A person acts with criminal negligence with respect to a result or to a circumstance described by a statute defining an offense when he fails to perceive a substantial and unjustifiable risk that such result will occur or that such circumstance exists. The risk must be of such nature and degree that the failure to perceive it constitutes a gross deviation from the standard of care that a reasonable person would observe in the situation."

§ 125.10 Criminally negligent homicide.

A person is guilty of criminally negligent homicide when, with criminal negligence, he causes the death of another person.

Criminally negligent homicide is a class E felony.

§ 125.11 Aggravated criminally negligent homicide.

A person is guilty of aggravated criminally negligent homicide when, with criminal negligence, he or she causes the death of a police officer or peace officer where such officer was in the course of performing his or her official duties and the defendant knew or reasonably should have known that such victim was a police officer or peace officer.

Aggravated criminally negligent homicide is a class C felony.

IV. Manslaughter

Comment: Vehicular manslaughter includes deaths caused while driving under the influence of intoxicates. First-degree manslaughter includes heat-of-passion homicides in which the defendant was acting under the influence of extreme emotional disturbance. Also included are incidents in which the defendant only intends to cause serious injury but death results.

Manslaughter in the second degree has the mental state of recklessness. Under statute 15.05 (3) of the Model Penal Code: "A person acts recklessly with respect to a result or to a circumstance described by a statute defining an offense when he is aware of and consciously disregards a substantial and unjustifiable risk that such result will occur or that such circumstance exists. The risk must be of such nature and degree that disregard thereof constitutes a gross deviation from the standard of conduct that a reasonable person would observe in the situation. A person who creates such a risk but is unaware thereof solely by reason of voluntary intoxication also acts recklessly with respect thereto."

§ 125.12 Vehicular manslaughter in the second degree.

A person is guilty of vehicular manslaughter in the second degree when he or she causes the death of another person, and either:

(1) operates a motor vehicle in violation of subdivision two, three, four or four-a of section eleven hundred ninety-two of the vehicle and traffic law or operates a vessel or public vessel in violation of paragraph (b), (c), (d) or (e) of subdivision two of section forty-nine-a of the

navigation law, and as a result of such intoxication or impairment by the use of a drug, or by the combined influence of drugs or of alcohol and any drug or drugs, operates such motor vehicle, vessel or public vessel in a manner that causes the death of such other person, or

(2) operates a motor vehicle with a gross vehicle weight rating of more than eighteen thousand pounds which contains flammable gas, radioactive materials or explosives in violation of subdivision one of section eleven hundred ninety-two of the vehicle and traffic law, and such flammable gas, radioactive materials or explosives is the cause of such death, and as a result of such impairment by the use of alcohol, operates such motor vehicle in a manner that causes the death of such other person, or

(3) operates a snowmobile in violation of paragraph (b), (c) or (d) of subdivision one of section 25.24 of the parks, recreation and historic preservation law or operates an all terrain vehicle as defined in paragraph (a) of subdivision one of section twenty-two hundred eighty-one of the vehicle and traffic law in violation of subdivision two, three, four, or four-a of section eleven hundred ninety-two of the vehicle and traffic law, and as a result of such intoxication or impairment by the use of a drug, or by the combined influence of drugs or of alcohol and any drug or drugs, operates such snowmobile or all terrain vehicle in a manner that causes the death of such other person. If it is established that the person operating such motor vehicle, vessel, public vessel, snowmobile or all terrain vehicle caused such death while unlawfully intoxicated or impaired by the use of alcohol or a drug, then there shall be a rebuttable presumption that, as a result of such intoxication or impairment by the use of alcohol or a drug, or by the combined influence of drugs or of alcohol and any drug or drugs, such person operated the motor vehicle, vessel, public vessel, snowmobile or all terrain vehicle in a manner that caused such death, as required by this section.

Vehicular manslaughter in the second degree is a class D felony.

§ 125.13 Vehicular manslaughter in the first degree.

A person is guilty of vehicular manslaughter in the first degree when he or she:

(1) commits the crime of vehicular manslaughter in the second degree as defined in section 125.12, and

(2) commits such crime while knowing or having reason to know that: (a) his or her license or his or her privilege of operating a motor vehicle in another state or his or her privilege of obtaining a license to operate a motor vehicle in another state is suspended or revoked and such suspension or revocation is based upon a conviction in such other state for an offense which would, if committed in this state, constitute a violation of any of the provisions of section eleven hundred ninety-two of the vehicle and traffic law; or (b) his or her license or his or her privilege of operating a motor vehicle in the state or his or her privilege of obtaining a license issued by the commissioner of motor vehicles is suspended or revoked and such suspension or revocation is based upon either a refusal to submit to a chemical test pursuant to section eleven hundred ninety-four of the vehicle and traffic law or following a conviction for a violation of any of the provisions of section eleven hundred ninety-two of the vehicle and traffic law.

If it is established that the person operating such motor vehicle caused such death while unlawfully intoxicated or impaired by the use of a drug, then there shall be a rebuttable presumption that, as a result of such intoxication or impairment by the use of a drug, such person operated the motor vehicle in a manner that caused such death, as required by this section.

Vehicular manslaughter in the first degree is a class C felony.

§ 125.20 Manslaughter in the first degree.

A person is guilty of manslaughter in the first degree when:

1. With intent to cause serious physical injury to another person, he causes the death of such person or of a third person; or

2. With intent to cause the death of another person, he causes the death of such person or of a third person under circumstances which do not constitute murder because he acts under the influence of extreme emotional disturbance, as defined in paragraph (a) of subdivision one of section 125.25. The fact that homicide was committed under the influence of extreme emotional disturbance constitutes a mitigating circumstance reducing murder to manslaughter in the first degree and need not be proved in any prosecution initiated under this subdivision; or

3. He commits upon a female pregnant for more than twenty-four weeks an abortional act which causes her death, unless such abortional act is justifiable pursuant to subdivision three of section 125.05; or

4. Being eighteen years old or more and with intent to cause physical injury to a person less than eleven years old, the defendant recklessly engages in conduct which creates a grave risk of serious physical injury to such person and thereby causes the death of such person.

Manslaughter in the first degree is a class B felony.

§ 125.22 Aggravated manslaughter in the first degree.

A person is guilty of aggravated manslaughter in the first degree when:

1. with intent to cause serious physical injury to a police officer or peace officer, where such officer was in the course of performing his or her official duties and the defendant knew or reasonably should have known that such victim was a police officer or a peace officer, he or she causes the death of such officer or another police officer or peace officer; or

2. with intent to cause the death of a police officer or peace officer, where such officer was in the course of performing his or her official duties and the defendant knew or reasonably should have known that such victim was a police officer or peace officer, he or she causes the death of such officer or another police officer or peace officer under circumstances which do not constitute murder because he or she acts under the influence of extreme emotional disturbance, as defined in paragraph (a) of subdivision one of section 125.25. The fact that homicide was committed under the influence of extreme emotional disturbance constitutes a mitigating circumstance reducing murder to aggravated manslaughter in the first degree or manslaughter in the first degree and need not be proved in any prosecution initiated under this subdivision.

Aggravated manslaughter in the first degree is a class B felony.

§ 125.15 Manslaughter in the second degree.

A person is guilty of manslaughter in the second degree when:

1. He recklessly causes the death of another person; or

2. He commits upon a female an abortional act which causes her death, unless such abortional act is justifiable pursuant to subdivision three of section 125.05; or

3. He intentionally causes or aids another person to commit suicide.

Manslaughter in the second degree is a class C felony.

§ 125.21 Aggravated manslaughter in the second degree.

A person is guilty of aggravated manslaughter in the second degree when he or she recklessly causes the death of a police officer or peace officer where such officer was in the course of performing his or her official duties and the defendant knew or reasonably should have known that such victim was a police officer or peace officer.

Aggravated manslaughter in the second degree is a class C felony.

V. Inducement to Commit Suicide and Assisted Suicide

***Comment*:** This statute addresses two issues concerning suicide. The first issue is in regards to when one person coerces another to commit suicide. There have been several publicized cases in which a victim has carried out the suicide act after being encouraged by another person. The key to a conviction is proving the suspect exercised substantial influence over the victim. If the victim survives the attempt they may be able to provide testimony. If the victim succeeds in the act, there may be no witness left.

The second concern addressed in the statute is the hotly debated issue of assisted suicide. The state of New York has outlawed the act of assisting the suicide of another individual. If anyone provides the physical means for another to commit suicide, or actually participates in the act, they are violation of the statute.

§ 120.30 Promoting a suicide attempt.

A person is guilty of promoting a suicide attempt when he intentionally causes or aids another person to attempt suicide.

Promoting a suicide attempt is a class E felony.

§ 120.35 Promoting a suicide attempt; when punishable as attempt to commit murder.

A person who engages in conduct constituting both the offense of promoting a suicide attempt and the offense of attempt to commit murder may not be convicted of attempt to commit murder unless he causes or aids the suicide attempt by the use of duress or deception.

Questions

1. After a long day at work, Ben returns home to discover his wife sleeping with his best friend. Outraged, Ben gets a gun from his dresser and kills his wife. What statute, if any, can be used to charge Ben with a crime? Would another statute apply if Ben had to drive to the gunshop and purchase the weapon before he killed his wife?

2. Veronica and her girlfriends go to a club and party until late that evening. When the bar closes, they all pile into her car and head home. Veronica is severely intoxicated and loses control of the vehicle, killing one of her passengers and injuring herself and the others. What statutes in this chapter, if any, apply to this incident?

3. Chad's wife is always threatening suicide, but he doesn't think she will actually kill herself. One day after she makes a threat, Chad loads his handgun, hands it to her, and tells her to go ahead. His wife takes the gun and kills herself. What statutes in this chapter, if any, apply to this incident?

4. Barb believes that if her boss is out of the way, she is next in line for a big promotion. She kills her supervisor and disposes of his body. Which statutes in this chapter, if any, can be used to obtain a conviction against Barb?

5. Terry is the driver of the get-away car for a bank robbery. During the robbery, one of the bank employees dies from a heart attack. Can Terry be charged with any other crimes besides robbery?

6. Mike hires Bob to kill the judge who presided over his divorce case. What degree of murder can the two men be charged with?

Chapter 7
Assault, Robbery, Rape, and Other Serious Crimes Against the Person

I. Menacing

***Comment*:** New York does not follow the traditional definitions of *assault* and *battery*. The state uses the term *menacing* to describe what the Model Penal Code refers to as *assault*. The elements of New York's menacing statutes match those of the Model Penal Code's crime of battery.

§ 120.13 Menacing in the first degree.

A person is guilty of menacing in the first degree when he or she commits the crime of menacing in the second degree and has been previously convicted of the crime of menacing in the second degree or the crime of menacing a police officer or peace officer within the preceding ten years.

Menacing in the first degree is a class E felony.

§ 120.14 Menacing in the second degree.

A person is guilty of menacing in the second degree when:

1. He or she intentionally places or attempts to place another person in reasonable fear of physical injury, serious physical injury or death by displaying a deadly weapon, dangerous instrument or what appears to be a pistol, revolver, rifle, shotgun, machine gun or other firearm; or

2. He or she repeatedly follows a person or engages in a course of conduct or repeatedly commits acts over a period of time intentionally placing or attempting to place another person in reasonable fear of physical injury, serious physical injury or death; or

3. He or she commits the crime of menacing in the third degree in violation of that part of a duly served order of protection, or such order which the defendant has actual knowledge of because he or she was present in court when such order was issued, pursuant to article eight of the family court act, section 530.12 of the criminal procedure law, or an order of protection issued by a court of competent jurisdiction in another state, territorial or tribal jurisdiction, which directed the respondent or defendant to stay away from the person or persons on whose behalf the order was issued.

Menacing in the second degree is a class A misdemeanor.

§ 120.15 Menacing in the third degree.

A person is guilty of menacing in the third degree when, by physical menace, he or she intentionally places or attempts to place another person in fear of death, imminent serious physical injury or physical injury.

Menacing in the third degree is a class B misdemeanor.

II. Assault (Battery)

Comment: An assault occurs when a person is physically touched in a harmful or insulting manner. The crime that an individual is charged with depends on the nature of the defendant's conduct, the amount of harm to the victim, whether a weapon was used, and the characteristics of the victim. New York statutes include three general degrees of assault and several statutes that protect certain types of victims.

§ 120.10 Assault in the first degree.

A person is guilty of assault in the first degree when:

1. With intent to cause serious physical injury to another person, he causes such injury to such person or to a third person by means of a deadly weapon or a dangerous instrument; or

2. With intent to disfigure another person seriously and permanently, or to destroy, amputate or disable permanently a member or organ of his body, he causes such injury to such person or to a third person; or

3. Under circumstances evincing a depraved indifference to human life, he recklessly engages in conduct which creates a grave risk of death to another person, and thereby causes serious physical injury to another person; or

4. In the course of and in furtherance of the commission or attempted commission of a felony or of immediate flight therefrom, he, or another participant if there be any, causes serious physical injury to a person other than one of the participants.

Assault in the first degree is a class B felony.

§ 120.05 Assault in the second degree.

A person is guilty of assault in the second degree when:

1. With intent to cause serious physical injury to another person, he causes such injury to such person or to a third person; or

2. With intent to cause physical injury to another person, he causes such injury to such person or to a third person by means of a deadly weapon or a dangerous instrument; or

3. With intent to prevent a peace officer, police officer, a fireman, including a fireman acting as a paramedic or emergency medical technician administering first aid in the course of performance of duty as such fireman, an emergency medical service paramedic or emergency medical service technician, or medical or related personnel in a hospital emergency department, from performing a lawful duty, by means including releasing or failing to control an animal under circumstances evincing the actor's intent that the animal obstruct the lawful activity of such peace officer, police officer, fireman, paramedic or technician, he causes physical injury to such peace officer, police officer, fireman, paramedic, technician or medical or related personnel in a hospital emergency department; or

4. He recklessly causes serious physical injury to another person by means of a deadly weapon or a dangerous instrument; or

5. For a purpose other than lawful medical or therapeutic treatment, he intentionally causes stupor, unconsciousness or other physical impairment or injury to another person by administering to him, without his consent, a drug, substance or preparation capable of producing the same; or

6. In the course of and in furtherance of the commission or attempted commission of a felony, other than a felony defined in article one hundred thirty which requires corroboration for conviction, or of immediate flight therefrom, he, or another participant if there be any, causes physical injury to a person other than one of the participants; or

7. Having been charged with or convicted of a crime and while confined in a correctional facility, as defined in subdivision three of section forty of the correction law, pursuant to such charge or conviction, with intent to cause physical injury to another person, he causes such injury to such person or to a third person; or

8. Being eighteen years old or more and with intent to cause physical injury to a person less than eleven years old, the defendant recklessly causes serious physical injury to such person; or

9. Being eighteen years old or more and with intent to cause physical injury to a person less than seven years old, the defendant causes such injury to such person; or

10. Acting at a place the person knows, or reasonably should know, is on school grounds and with intent to cause physical injury, he or she

(a) causes such injury to an employee of a school or public school district; or

(b) not being a student of such school or public school district, causes physical injury to another, and such other person is a student of such school who is attending or present for educational purposes. For purposes of this subdivision the term "school grounds" shall have the meaning set forth in subdivision fourteen of section 220.00 of this chapter.

11. With intent to cause physical injury to a train operator, ticket inspector, conductor, bus operator or station agent employed by any transit agency, authority or company, public or private, whose operation is authorized by New York state or any of its political subdivisions, he or she causes physical injury to such train operator, ticket inspector, conductor, bus operator or station agent while such employee is performing an assigned duty on, or directly related to, the operation of a train or bus.

Assault in the second degree is a class D felony.

§ 120.00 Assault in the third degree.

A person is guilty of assault in the third degree when:

1. With intent to cause physical injury to another person, he causes such injury to such person or to a third person; or

2. He recklessly causes physical injury to another person; or

3. With criminal negligence, he causes physical injury to another person by means of a deadly weapon or a dangerous instrument.

Assault in the third degree is a class A misdemeanor.

§ 120.12 Aggravated assault upon a person less than eleven years old.

A person is guilty of aggravated assault upon a person less than eleven years old when being eighteen years old or more the defendant commits the crime of assault in the third degree as defined in section 120.00 of this article upon a person less than eleven years old and has been previously convicted of such crime upon a person less than eleven years old within the preceding three years.

Aggravated assault upon a person less than eleven years old is a class E felony.

§ 120.11 Aggravated assault upon a police officer or a peace officer.

A person is guilty of aggravated assault upon a police officer or a peace officer when, with intent to cause serious physical injury to a person whom he knows or reasonably should know to be a police officer or a peace officer engaged in the course of performing his official duties, he causes such injury by means of a deadly weapon or dangerous instrument.

Aggravated assault upon a police officer or a peace officer is a class B felony.

III. Robbery

***Comments*:** New York robbery statutes include the traditional elements of robbery, such as the taking of property by threat or actual use of force. There are three degrees of robbery.

§ 160.00 Robbery; defined.

Robbery is forcible stealing. A person forcibly steals property and commits robbery when, in the course of committing a larceny, he uses or threatens the immediate use of physical force upon another person for the purpose of:

1. Preventing or overcoming resistance to the taking of the property or to the retention thereof immediately after the taking; or

2. Compelling the owner of such property or another person to deliver up the property or to engage in other conduct which aids in the commission of the larceny.

§ 160.15 Robbery in the first degree.

A person is guilty of robbery in the first degree when he forcibly steals property and when, in the course of the commission of the crime or of immediate flight therefrom, he or another participant in the crime:

1. Causes serious physical injury to any person who is not a participant in the crime; or

2. Is armed with a deadly weapon; or

3. Uses or threatens the immediate use of a dangerous instrument; or

4. Displays what appears to be a pistol, revolver, rifle, shotgun, machine gun or other firearm; except that in any prosecution under this subdivision, it is an affirmative defense that such pistol, revolver, rifle, shotgun, machine gun or other firearm was not a loaded weapon from which a

shot, readily capable of producing death or other serious physical injury, could be discharged. Nothing contained in this subdivision shall constitute a defense to a prosecution for, or preclude a conviction of, robbery in the second degree, robbery in the third degree or any other crime.

Robbery in the first degree is a class B felony.

§ 160.10 Robbery in the second degree.

A person is guilty of robbery in the second degree when he forcibly steals property and when:

1. He is aided by another person actually present; or

2. In the course of the commission of the crime or of immediate flight therefrom, he or another participant in the crime:

(a) Causes physical injury to any person who is not a participant in the crime; or

(b) Displays what appears to be a pistol, revolver, rifle, shotgun, machine gun or other firearm; or

3. The property consists of a motor vehicle, as defined in section one hundred twenty-five of the vehicle and traffic law.

Robbery in the second degree is a class C felony.

§ 160.05 Robbery in the third degree.

A person is guilty of robbery in the third degree when he forcibly steals property.

Robbery in the third degree is a class D felony.

IV. Rape and Sexual Crimes

Comment: New York Penal Law Article 130 contains 23 different sex offenses. The major offensives include several degrees of rape (forced sexual intercourse), criminal sexual acts (sodomy), and sexual abuse (sexual contact).

§ 130.00 Sex offenses; definitions of terms.

The following definitions are applicable to this article:

1. "Sexual intercourse" has its ordinary meaning and occurs upon any penetration, however slight.

2. (a) "Oral sexual conduct" means conduct between persons consisting of contact between the mouth and the penis, the mouth and the anus, or the mouth and the vulva or vagina.

(b) "Anal sexual conduct" means conduct between persons consisting of contact between the penis and anus.

3. "Sexual contact" means any touching of the sexual or other intimate parts of a person not married to the actor for the purpose of gratifying sexual desire of either party. It includes the

touching of the actor by the victim, as well as the touching of the victim by the actor, whether directly or through clothing.

4. For the purposes of this article "married" means the existence of the relationship between the actor and the victim as spouses which is recognized by law at the time the actor commits an offense proscribed by this article against the victim.

5. "Mentally disabled" means that a person suffers from a mental disease or defect which renders him or her incapable of appraising the nature of his or her conduct.

6. "Mentally incapacitated" means that a person is rendered temporarily incapable of appraising or controlling his conduct owing to the influence of a narcotic or intoxicating substance administered to him without his consent, or to any other act committed upon him without his consent.

7. "Physically helpless" means that a person is unconscious or for any other reason is physically unable to communicate unwillingness to an act.

8. "Forcible compulsion" means to compel by either:

a. use of physical force; or

b. a threat, express or implied, which places a person in fear of immediate death or physical injury to himself, herself or another person, or in fear that he, she or another person will immediately be kidnapped.

9. "Foreign object" means any instrument or article which, when inserted in the vagina, urethra, penis or rectum, is capable of causing physical injury.

10. "Sexual conduct" means sexual intercourse, oral sexual conduct, anal sexual conduct, aggravated sexual contact, or sexual contact.

11. "Aggravated sexual contact" means inserting, other than for a valid medical purpose, a foreign object in the vagina, urethra, penis or rectum of a child, thereby causing physical injury to such child.

12. "Health care provider" means any person who is, or is required to be, licensed or registered or holds himself or herself out to be licensed or registered, or provides services as if he or she were licensed or registered in the profession of medicine, chiropractic, dentistry or podiatry under any of the following: article one hundred thirty-one, one hundred thirty-two, one hundred thirty-three, or one hundred forty-one of the education law.

13. "Mental health care provider" shall mean a licensed physician, licensed psychologist, registered professional nurse, licensed clinical social worker or a licensed master social worker under the supervision of a physician, psychologist or licensed clinical social worker.

§ 130.05 Sex offenses; lack of consent.

1. Whether or not specifically stated, it is an element of every offense defined in this article that the sexual act was committed without consent of the victim.

2. Lack of consent results from:

(a) Forcible compulsion; or

(b) Incapacity to consent; or

(c) Where the offense charged is sexual abuse or forcible touching, any circumstances, in addition to forcible compulsion or incapacity to consent, in which the victim does not expressly or impliedly acquiesce in the actor's conduct; or

(d) Where the offense charged is rape in the third degree as defined in subdivision three of section 130.25, or criminal sexual act in the third degree as defined in subdivision three of section 130.40, in addition to forcible compulsion, circumstances under which, at the time of the act of intercourse, oral sexual conduct or anal sexual conduct, the victim clearly expressed that he or she did not consent to engage in such act, and a reasonable person in the actor's situation would have understood such person's words and acts as an expression of lack of consent to such act under all the circumstances.

3. A person is deemed incapable of consent when he or she is:

(a) less than seventeen years old; or

(b) mentally disabled; or

(c) mentally incapacitated; or

(d) physically helpless; or

(e) committed to the care and custody of the state department of correctional services or a hospital, as such term is defined in subdivision two of section four hundred of the correction law, and the actor is an employee, not married to such person, who knows or reasonably should know that such person is committed to the care and custody of such department or hospital. For purposes of this paragraph, "employee" means (i) an employee of the state department of correctional services who performs professional duties in a state correctional facility consisting of providing custody, medical or mental health services, counseling services, educational programs, or vocational training for inmates;

(ii) an employee of the division of parole who performs professional duties in a state correctional facility and who provides institutional parole services pursuant to section two hundred fifty-nine-e of the executive law; or

(iii) an employee of the office of mental health who performs professional duties in a state correctional facility or hospital, as such term is defined in subdivision two of section four hundred of the correction law, consisting of providing custody, or medical or mental health services for such inmates; or

(f) committed to the care and custody of a local correctional facility, as such term is defined in subdivision two of section forty of the correction law, and the actor is an employee, not married to such person, who knows or reasonably should know that such person is committed to the care and custody of such facility. For purposes of this paragraph, "employee" means an employee of the local correctional facility where the person is committed who performs professional duties consisting of providing custody, medical or mental health services, counseling services, educational services, or vocational training for inmates; or

(g) committed to or placed with the office of children and family services and in residential care, and the actor is an employee, not married to such person, who knows or reasonably should know that such person is committed to or placed with such office of children and family services and in residential care. For purposes of this paragraph, "employee" means an employee of the office of children and family services or of a residential facility who performs duties consisting of providing custody, medical or mental health services, counseling services, educational services, or vocational training for persons committed to or placed with the office of children and family services and in residential care; or

(h) a client or patient and the actor is a health care provider or mental health care provider charged with rape in the third degree as defined in section 130.25, criminal sexual act in the third degree as defined in section 130.40, aggravated sexual abuse in the fourth degree as defined in section 130.65-a, or sexual abuse in the third degree as defined in section 130.55, and the act of sexual conduct occurs during a treatment session, consultation, interview, or examination.

§ 130.10 Sex offenses; limitation; defenses.

1. In any prosecution under this article in which the victim's lack of consent is based solely upon his or her incapacity to consent because he or she was mentally disabled, mentally incapacitated or physically helpless, it is an affirmative defense that the defendant, at the time he or she engaged in the conduct constituting the offense, did not know of the facts or conditions responsible for such incapacity to consent.

2. Conduct performed for a valid medical or mental health care purpose shall not constitute a violation of any section of this article in which incapacity to consent is based on the circumstances set forth in paragraph (h) of subdivision three of section 130.05 of this article.

3. In any prosecution for the crime of rape in the third degree as defined in section 130.25, criminal sexual act in the third degree as defined in section 130.40, aggravated sexual abuse in the fourth degree as defined in section 130.65-a, or sexual abuse in the third degree as defined in section 130.55 in which incapacity to consent is based on the circumstances set forth in paragraph (h) of subdivision three of section 130. 05 of this article it shall be an affirmative defense that the client or patient consented to such conduct charged after having been expressly advised by the health care or mental health care provider that such conduct was not performed for a valid medical purpose.

4. In any prosecution under this article in which the victim's lack of consent is based solely on his or her incapacity to consent because he or she was less than seventeen years old, mentally disabled, or a client or patient and the actor is a health care provider, it shall be a defense that the defendant was married to the victim as defined in subdivision four of section 130.00 of this article.

§ 130.16 Sex offenses; corroboration.

A person shall not be convicted of any offense defined in this article of which lack of consent is an element but results solely from incapacity to consent because of the victim's mental defect, or mental incapacity, or an attempt to commit the same, solely on the testimony of the victim, unsupported by other evidence tending to:

(a) Establish that an attempt was made to engage the victim in sexual intercourse, oral sexual conduct, anal sexual conduct, or sexual contact, as the case may be, at the time of the occurrence; and

(b) Connect the defendant with the commission of the offense or attempted offense.

§ 130.20 Sexual misconduct.

A person is guilty of sexual misconduct when:

1. He or she engages in sexual intercourse with another person without such person's consent; or

2. He or she engages in oral sexual conduct or anal sexual conduct with another person without such person's consent; or

3. He or she engages in sexual conduct with an animal or a dead human body.

Sexual misconduct is a class A misdemeanor.

§ 130.35 Rape in the first degree.

A person is guilty of rape in the first degree when he or she engages in sexual intercourse with another person:

1. By forcible compulsion; or

2. Who is incapable of consent by reason of being physically helpless; or

3. Who is less than eleven years old; or

4. Who is less than thirteen years old and the actor is eighteen years old or more.

Rape in the first degree is a class B felony.

§ 130.30 Rape in the second degree.

A person is guilty of rape in the second degree when:

1. being eighteen years old or more, he or she engages in sexual intercourse with another person less than fifteen years old; or

2. he or she engages in sexual intercourse with another person who is incapable of consent by reason of being mentally disabled or mentally incapacitated.

It shall be an affirmative defense to the crime of rape in the second degree as defined in subdivision one of this section that the defendant was less than four years older than the victim at the time of the act.

Rape in the second degree is a class D felony.

§ 130.25 Rape in the third degree.

A person is guilty of rape in the third degree when:

1. He or she engages in sexual intercourse with another person who is incapable of consent by reason of some factor other than being less than seventeen years old;

2. Being twenty-one years old or more, he or she engages in sexual intercourse with another person less than seventeen years old; or

3. He or she engages in sexual intercourse with another person without such person's consent where such lack of consent is by reason of some factor other than incapacity to consent.

Rape in the third degree is a class E felony.

§ 130.50 Criminal sexual act in the first degree.

A person is guilty of criminal sexual act in the first degree when he or she engages in oral sexual conduct or anal sexual conduct with another person:

1. By forcible compulsion; or

2. Who is incapable of consent by reason of being physically helpless; or

3. Who is less than eleven years old; or

4. Who is less than thirteen years old and the actor is eighteen years old or more.

Criminal sexual act in the first degree is a class B felony.

§ 130.45 Criminal sexual act in the second degree.

A person is guilty of criminal sexual act in the second degree when:

1. being eighteen years old or more, he or she engages in oral sexual conduct or anal sexual conduct with another person less than fifteen years old; or

2. he or she engages in oral sexual conduct or anal sexual conduct with another person who is incapable of consent by reason of being mentally disabled or mentally incapacitated.

It shall be an affirmative defense to the crime of criminal sexual act in the second degree as defined in subdivision one of this section that the defendant was less than four years older than the victim at the time of the act.

Criminal sexual act in the second degree is a class D felony.

§ 130.40 Criminal sexual act in the third degree.

A person is guilty of criminal sexual act in the third degree when:

1. He or she engages in oral sexual conduct or anal sexual conduct with a person who is incapable of consent by reason of some factor other than being less than seventeen years old;

2. Being twenty-one years old or more, he or she engages in oral sexual conduct or anal sexual conduct with a person less than seventeen years old; or

3. He or she engages in oral sexual conduct or anal sexual conduct with another person without such person's consent where such lack of consent is by reason of some factor other than incapacity to consent.

Criminal sexual act in the third degree is a class E felony.

§ 130.52 Forcible touching.

A person is guilty of forcible touching when such person intentionally, and for no legitimate purpose, forcibly touches the sexual or other intimate parts of another person for the purpose of degrading or abusing such person; or for the purpose of gratifying the actor's sexual desire.

For the purposes of this section, forcible touching includes squeezing, grabbing or pinching.

Forcible touching is a class A misdemeanor.

§ 130.53 Persistent sexual abuse.

A person is guilty of persistent sexual abuse when he or she commits the crime of forcible touching, as defined in section 130.52 of this article, sexual abuse in the third degree, as defined in section 130.55 of this article, or sexual abuse in the second degree, as defined in section 130.60 of this article, and, within the previous ten year period, has been convicted two or more times, in separate criminal transactions for which sentence was imposed on separate occasions, of forcible touching, as defined in section 130.52 of this article, sexual abuse in the third degree as defined in section 130.55 of this article, sexual abuse in the second degree, as defined in section 130.60 of this article, or any offense defined in this article, of which the commission or attempted commission thereof is a felony.

Persistent sexual abuse is a class E felony.

§ 130.55 Sexual abuse in the third degree.

A person is guilty of sexual abuse in the third degree when he or she subjects another person to sexual contact without the latter's consent; except that in any prosecution under this section, it is an affirmative defense that (a) such other person's lack of consent was due solely to incapacity to consent by reason of being less than seventeen years old, and (b) such other person was more than fourteen years old, and (c) the defendant was less than five years older than such other person.

Sexual abuse in the third degree is a class B misdemeanor.

§ 130.60 Sexual abuse in the second degree.

A person is guilty of sexual abuse in the second degree when he or she subjects another person to sexual contact and when such other person is:

1. Incapable of consent by reason of some factor other than being less than seventeen years old; or

2. Less than fourteen years old.

Sexual abuse in the second degree is a class A misdemeanor.

§ 130.65 Sexual abuse in the first degree.

A person is guilty of sexual abuse in the first degree when he or she subjects another person to sexual contact:

1. By forcible compulsion; or

2. When the other person is incapable of consent by reason of being physically helpless; or

3. When the other person is less than eleven years old.

Sexual abuse in the first degree is a class D felony.

§ 130.70 Aggravated sexual abuse in the first degree.

1. A person is guilty of aggravated sexual abuse in the first degree when he inserts a foreign object in the vagina, urethra, penis or rectum of another person causing physical injury to such person:

(a) By forcible compulsion; or

(b) When the other person is incapable of consent by reason of being physically helpless; or

(c) When the other person is less than eleven years old.

2. Conduct performed for a valid medical purpose does not violate the provisions of this section.

Aggravated sexual abuse in the first degree is a class B felony.

§ 130.67 Aggravated sexual abuse in the second degree.

1. A person is guilty of aggravated sexual abuse in the second degree when he inserts a finger in the vagina, urethra, penis, or rectum of another person causing physical injury to such person:

(a) By forcible compulsion; or

(b) When the other person is incapable of consent by reason of being physically helpless; or

(c) When the other person is less than eleven years old.

2. Conduct performed for a valid medical purpose does not violate the provisions of this section.

Aggravated sexual abuse in the second degree is a class C felony.

§ 130.66 Aggravated sexual abuse in the third degree.

1. A person is guilty of aggravated sexual abuse in the third degree when he inserts a foreign object in the vagina, urethra, penis or rectum of another person:

(a) By forcible compulsion; or

(b) When the other person is incapable of consent by reason of being physically helpless; or

(c) When the other person is less than eleven years old.

2. A person is guilty of aggravated sexual abuse in the third degree when he or she inserts a foreign object in the vagina, urethra, penis or rectum of another person causing physical injury to

such person and such person is incapable of consent by reason of being mentally disabled or mentally incapacitated.

3. Conduct performed for a valid medical purpose does not violate the provisions of this section.

Aggravated sexual abuse in the third degree is a class D felony.

§ 130.65-A Aggravated sexual abuse in the fourth degree.

1. A person is guilty of aggravated sexual abuse in the fourth degree when

(a) He or she inserts a foreign object in the vagina, urethra, penis or rectum of another person and the other person is incapable of consent by reason of some factor other than being less than seventeen years old; or

(b) He or she inserts a finger in the vagina, urethra, penis or rectum of another person causing physical injury to such person and such person is incapable of consent by reason of some factor other than being less than seventeen years old.

2. Conduct performed for a valid medical purpose does not violate the provisions of this section

Aggravated sexual abuse in the fourth degree is a class E felony.

§ 130.75 Course of sexual conduct against a child in the first degree.

1. A person is guilty of course of sexual conduct against a child in the first degree when, over a period of time not less than three months in duration:

(a) he or she engages in two or more acts of sexual conduct, which includes at least one act of sexual intercourse, oral sexual conduct, anal sexual conduct or aggravated sexual contact, with a child less than eleven years old; or

(b) he or she, being eighteen years old or more, engages in two or more acts of sexual conduct, which include at least one act of sexual intercourse, oral sexual conduct, anal sexual conduct or aggravated sexual contact, with a child less than thirteen years old.

2. A person may not be subsequently prosecuted for any other sexual offense involving the same victim unless the other charged offense occurred outside the time period charged under this section.

Course of sexual conduct against a child in the first degree is a class B felony.

§ 130.80 Course of sexual conduct against a child in the second degree.

1. A person is guilty of course of sexual conduct against a child in the second degree when, over a period of time not less than three months in duration:

(a) he or she engages in two or more acts of sexual conduct with a child less than eleven years old; or

(b) he or she, being eighteen years old or more, engages in two or more acts of sexual conduct with a child less than thirteen years old.

2. A person may not be subsequently prosecuted for any other sexual offense involving the same victim unless the other charged offense occurred outside the time period charged under this section.

Course of sexual conduct against a child in the second degree is a class D felony.

Comments: Female genital mutilation is a cultural practice that was brought to the United States by immigrants from Africa and Asia. Typically, it is the victim's parents who arrange the procedure, because they believe that removing certain parts of the victim's genitals will stop the victim from becoming sexually immoral and dishonoring the family. The victims are usually preteens but can be infants or mature women.

§ 130.85 Female genital mutilation.

1. A person is guilty of female genital mutilation when:

(a) a person knowingly circumcises, excises, or infibulates the whole or any part of the labia majora or labia minora or clitoris of another person who has not reached eighteen years of age; or

(b) being a parent, guardian or other person legally responsible and charged with the care or custody of a child less than eighteen years old, he or she knowingly consents to the circumcision, excision or infibulation of whole or part of such child's labia majora or labia minora or clitoris.

2. Such circumcision, excision, or infibulation is not a violation of this section if such act is:

(a) necessary to the health of the person on whom it is performed, and is performed by a person licensed in the place of its performance as a medical practitioner; or

(b) performed on a person in labor or who has just given birth and is performed for medical purposes connected with that labor or birth by a person licensed in the place it is performed as a medical practitioner, midwife, or person in training to become such a practitioner or midwife.

3. For the purposes of paragraph (a) of subdivision two of this section, no account shall be taken of the effect on the person on whom such procedure is to be performed of any belief on the part of that or any other person that such procedure is required as a matter of custom or ritual.

Female genital mutilation is a class E felony.

§ 130.90 Facilitating a sex offense with a controlled substance.

A person is guilty of facilitating a sex offense with a controlled substance when he or she:

1. knowingly and unlawfully possesses a controlled substance or any preparation, compound, mixture or substance that requires a prescription to obtain and administers such substance or preparation, compound, mixture or substance that requires a prescription to obtain to another person without such person's consent and with intent to commit against such person conduct constituting a felony defined in this article; and

2. commits or attempts to commit such conduct constituting a felony defined in this article.

Facilitating a sex offense with a controlled substance is a class D felony.

§ 130.95 Predatory sexual assault.

A person is guilty of predatory sexual assault when he or she commits the crime of rape in the first degree, criminal sexual act in the first degree, aggravated sexual abuse in the first degree, or course of sexual conduct against a child in the first degree, as defined in this article, and when:

1. In the course of the commission of the crime or the immediate flight therefrom, he or she:

(a) Causes serious physical injury to the victim of such crime; or

(b) Uses or threatens the immediate use of a dangerous instrument; or

2. He or she has engaged in conduct constituting the crime of rapc in the first degree, criminal sexual act in the first degree, aggravated sexual abuse in the first degree, or course of sexual conduct against a child in the first degree, as defined in this article, against one or more additional persons; or

3. He or she has previously been subjected to a conviction for a felony defined in this article, incest as defined in section 255.25 of this chapter or use of a child in a sexual performance as defined in section 263.05 of this chapter.

Predatory sexual assault is a class A-II felony.

§ 130.96 Predatory sexual assault against a child.

A person is guilty of predatory sexual assault against a child when, being eighteen years old or more, he or she commits the crime of rape in the first degree, criminal sexual act in the first degree, aggravated sexual abuse in the first degree, or course of sexual conduct against a child in the first degree, as defined in this article, and the victim is less than thirteen years old.

Predatory sexual assault against a child is a class A-II felony.

V. Incest

Comment: Incest is limited to sexual acts between parents and children, between siblings, and between other directly related relatives such as aunts and uncles and their nieces and nephews.

§ 255.25 Incest.

A person is guilty of incest when he or she marries or engages in sexual intercourse, oral sexual conduct or anal sexual conduct with a person whom he or she knows to be related to him or her, either legitimately or out of wedlock, as an ancestor, descendant, brother or sister of either the whole or the half blood, uncle, aunt, nephew or niece.

Incest is a class E felony.

§ 255.30 Adultery and incest; corroboration.

1. A person shall not be convicted of adultery or of an attempt to commit adultery solely upon the testimony of the other party to the adulterous act or attempted act, unsupported by other

evidence tending to establish that the defendant attempted to engage with the other party in sexual intercourse, and that the defendant or the other party had a living spouse at the time of the adulterous act or attempted act.

2. A person shall not be convicted of incest or of an attempt to commit incest solely upon the testimony of the other party unsupported by other evidence tending to establish that the defendant married the other party, or that the defendant was a relative of the other party of a kind specified in section 255.25.

VI. False Imprisonment and Kidnapping

***Comment*:** A typical unlawful restraint incident involves a situation in which a person is temporarily held against his or her will. Kidnapping occurs when an individual restrains—with or without the use or threat of deadly force—another person and secretly confines the victim in a place that he or she will not be discovered.

§ 135.00 Unlawful imprisonment, kidnapping and custodial interference; definitions of terms.

The following definitions are applicable to this article:

1. "Restrain" means to restrict a person's movements intentionally and unlawfully in such manner as to interfere substantially with his liberty by moving him from one place to another, or by confining him either in the place where the restriction commences or in a place to which he has been moved, without consent and with knowledge that the restriction is unlawful. A person is so moved or confined "without consent" when such is accomplished by (a) physical force, intimidation or deception, or (b) any means whatever, including acquiescence of the victim, if he is a child less than sixteen years old or an incompetent person and the parent, guardian or other person or institution having lawful control or custody of him has not acquiesced in the movement or confinement.

2. "Abduct" means to restrain a person with intent to prevent his liberation by either (a) secreting or holding him in a place where he is not likely to be found, or (b) using or threatening to use deadly physical force.

3. "Relative" means a parent, ancestor, brother, sister, uncle or aunt.

§ 135.10 Unlawful imprisonment in the first degree.

A person is guilty of unlawful imprisonment in the first degree when he restrains another person under circumstances which expose the latter to a risk of serious physical injury.

Unlawful imprisonment in the first degree is a class E felony.

§ 135.05 Unlawful imprisonment in the second degree.

A person is guilty of unlawful imprisonment in the second degree when he restrains another person.

Unlawful imprisonment in the second degree is a class A misdemeanor.

§ 135.15 Unlawful imprisonment; defense.

In any prosecution for unlawful imprisonment, it is an affirmative defense that (a) the person restrained was a child less than sixteen years old, and (b) the defendant was a relative of such child, and (c) his sole purpose was to assume control of such child.

§ 135.25 Kidnapping in the first degree.

A person is guilty of kidnapping in the first degree when he abducts another person and when:

1. His intent is to compel a third person to pay or deliver money or property as ransom, or to engage in other particular conduct, or to refrain from engaging in particular conduct; or

2. He restrains the person abducted for a period of more than twelve hours with intent to:

(a) Inflict physical injury upon him or violate or abuse him sexually; or

(b) Accomplish or advance the commission of a felony; or

(c) Terrorize him or a third person; or

(d) Interfere with the performance of a governmental or political function; or

3. The person abducted dies during the abduction or before he is able to return or to be returned to safety. Such death shall be presumed, in a case where such person was less than sixteen years old or an incompetent person at the time of the abduction, from evidence that his parents, guardians or other lawful custodians did not see or hear from him following the termination of the abduction and prior to trial and received no reliable information during such period persuasively indicating that he was alive. In all other cases, such death shall be presumed from evidence that a person whom the person abducted would have been extremely likely to visit or communicate with during the specified period were he alive and free to do so did not see or hear from him during such period and received no reliable information during such period persuasively indicating that he was alive.

Kidnapping in the first degree is a class A-I felony.

§ 135.20 Kidnapping in the second degree.

A person is guilty of kidnapping in the second degree when he abducts another person.

Kidnapping in the second degree is a class B felony.

§ 135.30 Kidnapping; defense.

In any prosecution for kidnapping, it is an affirmative defense that (a) the defendant was a relative of the person abducted, and (b) his sole purpose was to assume control of such person.

VII. Stalking

Comments: Stalking is a crime based on a suspect's harassment of a victim. One of the main aspects of stalking is that the suspect must place the victim in apprehension of immediate or future harm.

§ 120.45 Stalking in the fourth degree.

A person is guilty of stalking in the fourth degree when he or she intentionally, and for no legitimate purpose, engages in a course of conduct directed at a specific person, and knows or reasonably should know that such conduct:

1. is likely to cause reasonable fear of material harm to the physical health, safety or property of such person, a member of such person's immediate family or a third party with whom such person is acquainted; or

2. causes material harm to the mental or emotional health of such person, where such conduct consists of following, telephoning or initiating communication or contact with such person, a member of such person's immediate family or a third party with whom such person is acquainted, and the actor was previously clearly informed to cease that conduct; or

3. is likely to cause such person to reasonably fear that his or her employment, business or career is threatened, where such conduct consists of appearing, telephoning or initiating communication or contact at such person's place of employment or business, and the actor was previously clearly informed to cease that conduct.

Stalking in the fourth degree is a class B misdemeanor.

§ 120.50 Stalking in the third degree.

A person is guilty of stalking in the third degree when he or she:

1. Commits the crime of stalking in the fourth degree in violation of section 120.45 of this article against three or more persons, in three or more separate transactions, for which the actor has not been previously convicted; or

2. Commits the crime of stalking in the fourth degree in violation of section 120.45 of this article against any person, and has previously been convicted, within the preceding ten years of a specified predicate crime, as defined in subdivision five of section 120.40 of this article, and the victim of such specified predicate crime is the victim, or an immediate family member of the victim, of the present offense; or

3. With intent to harass, annoy or alarm a specific person, intentionally engages in a course of conduct directed at such person which is likely to cause such person to reasonably fear physical injury or serious physical injury, the commission of a sex offense against, or the kidnapping, unlawful imprisonment or death of such person or a member of such person's immediate family; or

4. Commits the crime of stalking in the fourth degree and has previously been convicted within the preceding ten years of stalking in the fourth degree.

Stalking in the third degree is a class A misdemeanor.

§ 120.55 Stalking in the second degree.

A person is guilty of stalking in the second degree when he or she:

1. Commits the crime of stalking in the third degree as defined in subdivision three of section 120.50 of this article and in the course of and in furtherance of the commission of such offense: (i) displays, or possesses and threatens the use of, a firearm, pistol, revolver, rifle, shotgun, machine gun, electronic dart gun, electronic stun gun, cane sword, billy, blackjack, bludgeon, metal knuckles, chuka stick, sand bag, sandclub, slingshot, slungshot, shirken, "Kung Fu Star", dagger, dangerous knife, dirk, razor, stiletto, imitation pistol, dangerous instrument, deadly instrument or deadly weapon; or (ii) displays what appears to be a pistol, revolver, rifle, shotgun, machine gun or other firearm; or

2. Commits the crime of stalking in the third degree in violation of subdivision three of section 120.50 of this article against any person, and has previously been convicted, within the preceding five years, of a specified predicate crime as defined in subdivision five of section 120.40 of this article, and the victim of such specified predicate crime is the victim, or an immediate family member of the victim, of the present offense; or

3. Commits the crime of stalking in the fourth degree and has previously been convicted of stalking in the third degree as defined in subdivision four of section 120.50 of this article against any person; or

4. Being twenty-one years of age or older, repeatedly follows a person under the age of fourteen or engages in a course of conduct or repeatedly commits acts over a period of time intentionally placing or attempting to place such person who is under the age of fourteen in reasonable fear of physical injury, serious physical injury or death; or

5. Commits the crime of stalking in the third degree, as defined in subdivision three of section 120.50 of this article, against ten or more persons, in ten or more separate transactions, for which the actor has not been previously convicted.

Stalking in the second degree is a class E felony.

§ 120.60 Stalking in the first degree.

A person is guilty of stalking in the first degree when he or she commits the crime of stalking in the third degree as defined in subdivision three of section 120.50 or stalking in the second degree as defined in section 120.55 of this article and, in the course and furtherance thereof, he or she:

1. intentionally or recklessly causes physical injury to the victim of such crime; or

2. commits a class A misdemeanor defined in article one hundred thirty of this chapter, or a class E felony defined in section 130.25, 130.40 or 130.85 of this chapter, or a class D felony defined in section 130.30 or 130.45 of this chapter.

Stalking in the first degree is a class D felony.

§ 240.25 Harassment in the first degree.

A person is guilty of harassment in the first degree when he or she intentionally and repeatedly harasses another person by following such person in or about a public place or places or by engaging in a course of conduct or by repeatedly committing acts which places such person in reasonable fear of physical injury. This section shall not apply to activities regulated by the national labor relations act, as amended, the railway labor act, as amended, or the federal employment labor management act, as amended.

Harassment in the first degree is a class B misdemeanor.

§ 240.31 Aggravated harassment in the first degree.

A person is guilty of aggravated harassment in the first degree when with intent to harass, annoy, threaten or alarm another person, because of a belief or perception regarding such person's race, color, national origin, ancestry, gender, religion, religious practice, age, disability or sexual orientation, regardless of whether the belief or perception is correct, he or she:

1. Damages premises primarily used for religious purposes, or acquired pursuant to section six of the religious corporation law and maintained for purposes of religious instruction, and the damage to the premises exceeds fifty dollars; or

2. Commits the crime of aggravated harassment in the second degree in the manner proscribed by the provisions of subdivision three of section 240.30 of this article and has been previously convicted of the crime of aggravated harassment in the second degree for the commission of conduct proscribed by the provisions of subdivision three of section 240.30 or he has been previously convicted of the crime of aggravated harassment in the first degree within the preceding ten years.

Aggravated harassment in the first degree is a class E felony.

VIII. Hate Crimes

***Comments*:** Hate crime statutes are a response to concerns regarding crimes motivated by a victim's characteristics. A hate crime occurs when one of the suspect's motivating factors for committing the crime falls within the categories listed in the statutes below.

§ 485.00 Legislative findings.

The legislature finds and determines as follows: criminal acts involving violence, intimidation and destruction of property based upon bias and prejudice have become more prevalent in New York state in recent years. The intolerable truth is that in these crimes, commonly and justly referred to as "hate crimes", victims are intentionally selected, in whole or in part, because of their race, color, national origin, ancestry, gender, religion, religious practice, age, disability or sexual orientation. Hate crimes do more than threaten the safety and welfare of all citizens. They inflict on victims incalculable physical and emotional damage and tear at the very fabric of free society. Crimes motivated by invidious hatred toward particular groups not only harm individual victims but send a powerful message of intolerance and discrimination to all members of the group to which the victim belongs. Hate crimes can and do intimidate and disrupt entire communities and vitiate the civility that is essential to healthy democratic processes. In a democratic society, citizens cannot be required to approve of the beliefs and practices of others, but must never commit criminal acts on account of them. Current law does not adequately recognize the harm to public order and individual safety that hate crimes cause. Therefore, our laws must be strengthened to provide clear recognition of the gravity of hate crimes and the compelling importance of preventing their recurrence.

Accordingly, the legislature finds and declares that hate crimes should be prosecuted and punished with appropriate severity.

§ 485.05 Hate crimes.

1. A person commits a hate crime when he or she commits a specified offense and either:

(a) intentionally selects the person against whom the offense is committed or intended to be committed in whole or in substantial part because of a belief or perception regarding the race, color, national origin, ancestry, gender, religion, religious practice, age, disability or sexual orientation of a person, regardless of whether the belief or perception is correct, or

(b) intentionally commits the act or acts constituting the offense in whole or in substantial part because of a belief or perception regarding the race, color, national origin, ancestry, gender, religion, religious practice, age, disability or sexual orientation of a person, regardless of whether the belief or perception is correct.

2. Proof of race, color, national origin, ancestry, gender, religion, religious practice, age, disability or sexual orientation of the defendant, the victim or of both the defendant and the victim does not, by itself, constitute legally sufficient evidence satisfying the people's burden under paragraph (a) or (b) of subdivision one of this section.

3. A "specified offense" is an offense defined by any of the following provisions of this chapter: section 120.00 (assault in the third degree); section 120.05 (assault in the second degree); section 120.10 (assault in the first degree); section 120.12 (aggravated assault upon a person less than eleven years old); section 120.13 (menacing in the first degree); section 120.14 (menacing in the second degree); section 120. 15 (menacing in the third degree); section 120.20 (reckless endangerment in the second degree); section 120.25 (reckless endangerment in the first degree); subdivision one of section 125.15 (manslaughter in the second degree); subdivision one, two or four of section 125.20 (manslaughter in the first degree); section 125.25 (murder in the second degree); section 120.45 (stalking in the fourth degree); section 120.50 (stalking in the third degree); section 120.55 (stalking in the second degree); section 120. 60 (stalking in the first degree); subdivision one of section 130.35 (rape in the first degree); subdivision one of section 130.50 (criminal sexual act in the first degree); subdivision one of section 130.65 (sexual abuse in the first degree); paragraph (a) of subdivision one of section 130.67 (aggravated sexual abuse in the second degree); paragraph (a) of subdivision one of section 130.70 (aggravated sexual abuse in the first degree); section 135.05 (unlawful imprisonment in the second degree); section 135.10 (unlawful imprisonment in the first degree); section 135.20 (kidnapping in the second degree); section 135.25 (kidnapping in the first degree); section 135.60 (coercion in the second degree); section 135.65 (coercion in the first degree); section 140.10 (criminal trespass in the third degree); section 140.15 (criminal trespass in the second degree); section 140.17 (criminal

trespass in the first degree); section 140.20 (burglary in the third degree); section 140.25 (burglary in the second degree); section 140.30 (burglary in the first degree); section 145.00 (criminal mischief in the fourth degree); section 145.05 (criminal mischief in the third degree); section 145.10 (criminal mischief in the second degree); section 145.12 (criminal mischief in the first degree); section 150.05 (arson in the fourth degree); section 150.10 (arson in the third degree); section 150.15 (arson in the second degree); section 150.20 (arson in the first degree); section 155.25 (petit larceny); section 155.30 (grand larceny in the fourth degree); section 155.35 (grand larceny in the third degree); section 155.40 (grand larceny in the second degree); section 155.42 (grand larceny in the first degree); section 160.05 (robbery in the third degree); section 160.10 (robbery in the second degree); \fs24ulsection 160.15 (robbery in the first degree); section 240.25 (harassment in the first degree); subdivision one, two or four of section 240.30 (aggravated harassment in the second degree); or any attempt or conspiracy to commit any of the foregoing offenses.

4. For purposes of this section:

(a) the term "age" means sixty years old or more;

(b) the term "disability" means a physical or mental impairment that substantially limits a major life activity.

§ 485.10 Sentencing.

1. When a person is convicted of a hate crime pursuant to this article, and the specified offense is a violent felony offense, as defined in section 70.02 of this chapter, the hate crime shall be deemed a violent felony offense.

2. When a person is convicted of a hate crime pursuant to this article and the specified offense is a misdemeanor or a class C, D or E felony, the hate crime shall be deemed to be one category higher than the specified offense the defendant committed, or one category higher than the offense level applicable to the defendant's conviction for an attempt or conspiracy to commit a specified offense, whichever is applicable.

3. Notwithstanding any other provision of law, when a person is convicted of a hate crime pursuant to this article and the specified offense is a class B felony:

(a) the maximum term of the indeterminate sentence must be at least six years if the defendant is sentenced pursuant to section 70.00 of this chapter;

(b) the term of the determinate sentence must be at least eight years if the defendant is sentenced pursuant to section 70.02 of this chapter;

(c) the term of the determinate sentence must be at least twelve years if the defendant is sentenced pursuant to section 70.04 of this chapter;

(d) the maximum term of the indeterminate sentence must be at least four years if the defendant is sentenced pursuant to section 70.05 of this chapter; and

(e) the maximum term of the indeterminate sentence or the term of the determinate sentence must be at least ten years if the defendant is sentenced pursuant to section 70.06 of this chapter.

4. Notwithstanding any other provision of law, when a person is convicted of a hate crime pursuant to this article and the specified offense is a class A-1 felony, the minimum period of the indeterminate sentence shall be not less than twenty years.

Questions

1. Shawn and Kelly have just spent a wonderful evening together. Shawn decides he wants to have sex with Kelly and begins kissing her and touching her. She tells him that she is not ready to take that step in the relationship with him. He gets angry and forces her to have intercourse with him. What statutes in this chapter, if any, apply to this incident? Would it matter if Kelly were able to talk Shawn into using a condom?

2. Rick and his girlfriend Marsha are at a concert when another man begins flirting with her. Rick gets angry, starts hitting the man, and is arrested for his actions. What statutes in this chapter, if any, apply to this incident? Does it matter whether or not Rick uses his fists or a beer bottle?

3. Jill has reported her brother to the authorities for sexually abusing her daughter several times. The authorities investigate and determine he has had sexual intercourse with the child. What statutes in this chapter, if any, apply to this incident?

4. Mary arrives home to discover her 40-year-old neighbor French kissing her 15-year-old daughter. The neighbor claims he did not force Mary's daughter and that there was no other contact besides the kiss. The daughter reaffirms the neighbor's story, but Mary calls the police. What statutes in this chapter, if any, apply to this incident?

5. Todd is hungry, but he has no money. He decides to order a pizza and use the empty house down the street as the delivery address. When the pizza deliveryman arrives, Todd knocks him down and flees with the pizza. What statutes, if any, is Todd in violation of?

6. Tom plays an online computer action game. Several times a week, another player Hank gets mad at Tom for not playing well. The two players exchange insults in the game's chatroom, and Hank threatens to hunt Tom down and kill him. Hank soon begins to send emails to Tom, clearly describing Tom's house and warning him not to leave it. What statutes in this chapter, if any, apply to this incident?

7. A white supremacy group holds monthly meetings in town. The group decides to send letters to all the nonwhite people in town telling them to move out of the area. The letters contain no actual threats. What statutes, if any, have the group violated?

8. Susan locks her 18-year-old daughter in her room. Due to the locks on the door and the bars on the window, her daughter cannot escape. What statutes, if any, have Susan violated?

9. Janet is a corrections officer, and one of the inmates she supervises is Brian. One day while she is walking by his cell, he throws a cup of urine on her. Has Brian violated a statute?

Chapter 8
Property and Related Crimes

I. Larceny

***Comment*:** Theft crimes are classified as *petit theft* or as one of the four degrees of grand larceny. Petit theft is a misdemeanor, and grand theft is a felony. In determining which crime to charge, the prosecutor examines the nature of the theft and the value of the stolen goods. Subsection two of the second degree grand larceny statute allows for special consideration of the characteristics and actions of the defendant.

§ 155.00 Larceny; definitions of terms.

The following definitions are applicable to this title:

1. "Property" means any money, personal property, real property, computer data, computer program, thing in action, evidence of debt or contract, or any article, substance or thing of value, including any gas, steam, water or electricity, which is provided for a charge or compensation.

2. "Obtain" includes, but is not limited to, the bringing about of a transfer or purported transfer of property or of a legal interest therein, whether to the obtainer or another.

3. "Deprive." To "deprive" another of property means (a) to withhold it or cause it to be withheld from him permanently or for so extended a period or under such circumstances that the major portion of its economic value or benefit is lost to him, or (b) to dispose of the property in such manner or under such circumstances as to render it unlikely that an owner will recover such property.

4. "Appropriate." To "appropriate" property of another to oneself or a third person means (a) to exercise control over it, or to aid a third person to exercise control over it, permanently or for so extended a period or under such circumstances as to acquire the major portion of its economic value or benefit, or (b) to dispose of the property for the benefit of oneself or a third person.

5. "Owner." When property is taken, obtained or withheld by one person from another person, an "owner" thereof means any person who has a right to possession thereof superior to that of the taker, obtainer or withholder.

A person who has obtained possession of property by theft or other illegal means shall be deemed to have a right of possession superior to that of a person who takes, obtains or withholds it from him by larcenous means.

A joint or common owner of property shall not be deemed to have a right of possession thereto superior to that of any other joint or common owner thereof.

In the absence of a specific agreement to the contrary, a person in lawful possession of property shall be deemed to have a right of possession superior to that of a person having only a security interest therein, even if legal title lies with the holder of the security interest pursuant to a conditional sale contract or other security agreement.

6. “Secret scientific material” means a sample, culture, micro-organism, specimen, record, recording, document, drawing or any other article, material, device or substance which constitutes, represents, evidences, reflects, or records a scientific or technical process, invention or formula or any part or phase thereof, and which is not, and is not intended to be, available to anyone other than the person or persons rightfully in possession thereof or selected persons having access thereto with his or their consent, and when it accords or may accord such rightful possessors an advantage over competitors or other persons who do not have knowledge or the benefit thereof.

7. “Credit card” means any instrument or article defined as a credit card in section five hundred eleven of the general business law.

7-a. “Debit card” means any instrument or article defined as a debit card in section five hundred eleven of the general business law.

7-b. “Public benefit card” means any medical assistance card, food stamp assistance card, public assistance card, or any other identification, authorization card or electronic access device issued by the state or a social services district as defined in subdivision seven of section two of the social services law, which entitles a person to obtain public assistance benefits under a local, state or federal program administered by the state, its political subdivisions or social services districts.

7-c. “Access device” means any telephone calling card number, credit card number, account number, mobile identification number, electronic serial number or personal identification number that can be used to obtain telephone service.

8. “Service” includes, but is not limited to, labor, professional service, a computer service, transportation service, the supplying of hotel accommodations, restaurant services, entertainment, the supplying of equipment for use, and the supplying of commodities of a public utility nature such as gas, electricity, steam and water. A ticket or equivalent instrument which evidences a right to receive a service is not in itself service but constitutes property within the meaning of subdivision one.

9. “Cable television service” means any and all services provided by or through the facilities of any cable television system or closed circuit coaxial cable communications system, or any microwave or similar transmission service used in connection with any cable television system or other similar closed circuit coaxial cable communications system.

§ 155.05 Larceny; defined.

1. A person steals property and commits larceny when, with intent to deprive another of property or to appropriate the same to himself or to a third person, he wrongfully takes, obtains or withholds such property from an owner thereof.

2. Larceny includes a wrongful taking, obtaining or withholding of another’s property, with the intent prescribed in subdivision one of this section, committed in any of the following ways:

(a) By conduct heretofore defined or known as common law larceny by trespassory taking, common law larceny by trick, embezzlement, or obtaining property by false pretenses;

(b) By acquiring lost property.

A person acquires lost property when he exercises control over property of another which he knows to have been lost or mislaid, or to have been delivered under a mistake as to the identity of the recipient or the nature or amount of the property, without taking reasonable measures to return such property to the owner;

(c) By committing the crime of issuing a bad check, as defined in section 190.05;

(d) By false promise.

A person obtains property by false promise when, pursuant to a scheme to defraud, he obtains property of another by means of a representation, express or implied, that he or a third person will in the future engage in particular conduct, and when he does not intend to engage in such conduct or, as the case may be, does not believe that the third person intends to engage in such conduct.

In any prosecution for larceny based upon a false promise, the defendant's intention or belief that the promise would not be performed may not be established by or inferred from the fact alone that such promise was not performed. Such a finding may be based only upon evidence establishing that the facts and circumstances of the case are wholly consistent with guilty intent or belief and wholly inconsistent with innocent intent or belief, and excluding to a moral certainty every hypothesis except that of the defendant's intention or belief that the promise would not be performed;

(e) By extortion.

A person obtains property by extortion when he compels or induces another person to deliver such property to himself or to a third person by means of instilling in him a fear that, if the property is not so delivered, the actor or another will:

(i) Cause physical injury to some person in the future; or

(ii) Cause damage to property; or

(iii) Engage in other conduct constituting a crime; or

(iv) Accuse some person of a crime or cause criminal charges to be instituted against him; or

(v) Expose a secret or publicize an asserted fact, whether true or false, tending to subject some person to hatred, contempt or ridicule; or

(vi) Cause a strike, boycott or other collective labor group action injurious to some person's business; except that such a threat shall not be deemed extortion when the property is demanded or received for the benefit of the group in whose interest the actor purports to act; or

(vii) Testify or provide information or withhold testimony or information with respect to another's legal claim or defense; or

(viii) Use or abuse his position as a public servant by performing some act within or related to his official duties, or by failing or refusing to perform an official duty, in such manner as to affect some person adversely; or

(ix) Perform any other act which would not in itself materially benefit the actor but which is calculated to harm another person materially with respect to his health, safety, business, calling, career, financial condition, reputation or personal relationships.

§ 155.25 Petit larceny.

A person is guilty of petit larceny when he steals property.

Petit larceny is a class A misdemeanor.

§ 155.30 Grand larceny in the fourth degree.

A person is guilty of grand larceny in the fourth degree when he steals property and when:

1. The value of the property exceeds one thousand dollars; or

2. The property consists of a public record, writing or instrument kept, filed or deposited according to law with or in the keeping of any public office or public servant; or

3. The property consists of secret scientific material; or

4. The property consists of a credit card or debit card; or

5. The property, regardless of its nature and value, is taken from the person of another; or

6. The property, regardless of its nature and value, is obtained by extortion; or

7. The property consists of one or more firearms, rifles or shotguns, as such terms are defined in section 265.00 of this chapter; or

8. The value of the property exceeds one hundred dollars and the property consists of a motor vehicle, as defined in section one hundred twenty-five of the vehicle and traffic law, other than a motorcycle, as defined in section one hundred twenty-three of such law; or

9. The property consists of a scroll, religious vestment, vessel or other item of property having a value of at least one hundred dollars kept for or used in connection with religious worship in any building or structure used as a place of religious worship by a religious corporation, as incorporated under the religious corporations law or the education law.

10. The property consists of an access device which the person intends to use unlawfully to obtain telephone service.

11. The property consists of anhydrous ammonia or liquified ammonia gas and the actor intends to use, or knows another person intends to use, such anhydrous ammonia or liquified ammonia gas to manufacture methamphetamine.

Grand larceny in the fourth degree is a class E felony.

§ 155.35 Grand larceny in the third degree.

A person is guilty of grand larceny in the third degree when he steals property and when the value of the property exceeds three thousand dollars.

Grand larceny in the third degree is a class D felony.

§ 155.40 Grand larceny in the second degree.

A person is guilty of grand larceny in the second degree when he steals property and when:

1. The value of the property exceeds fifty thousand dollars; or

2. The property, regardless of its nature and value, is obtained by extortion committed by instilling in the victim a fear that the actor or another person will (a) cause physical injury to some person in the future, or (b) cause damage to property, or (c) use or abuse his position as a public servant by engaging in conduct within or related to his official duties, or by failing or refusing to perform an official duty, in such manner as to affect some person adversely.

Grand larceny in the second degree is a class C felony.

§ 155.42 Grand larceny in the first degree.

A person is guilty of grand larceny in the first degree when he steals property and when the value of the property exceeds one million dollars.

Grand larceny in the first degree is a class B felony.

II. Burglary

***Comment*:** Burglary is divided into three degrees and is punishable as a class B felony, class C felony, or a class D felony. A required element of common law burglary was that the crime must have taken place in a dwelling. Burglary of a home continues to be treated as a serious violation, and, depending on the circumstances, the offense can be either a first-degree or second degree burglary.

New York extends the crime of burglary to cover unlawful entry into vehicles, aircraft, and boats that are used for lodging. By defining such vehicles as "buildings" in statute 140.00 (2), a burglary of these vehicles is a class D felony under the third-degree burglary statute.

§ 140.00 Criminal trespass and burglary; definitions of terms.

The following definitions are applicable to this article:

1. "Premises" includes the term "building," as defined herein, and any real property.

2. "Building," in addition to its ordinary meaning, includes any structure, vehicle or watercraft used for overnight lodging of persons, or used by persons for carrying on business therein, or used as an elementary or secondary school, or an inclosed motor truck, or an inclosed motor truck trailer. Where a building consists of two or more units separately secured or occupied, each unit shall be deemed both a separate building in itself and a part of the main building.

3. "Dwelling" means a building which is usually occupied by a person lodging therein at night.

4. "Night" means the period between thirty minutes after sunset and thirty minutes before sunrise.

5. "Enter or remain unlawfully." A person "enters or remains unlawfully" in or upon premises when he is not licensed or privileged to do so. A person who, regardless of his intent, enters or remains in or upon premises which are at the time open to the public does so with license and privilege unless he defies a lawful order not to enter or remain, personally communicated to him by the owner of such premises or other authorized person. A license or privilege to enter or remain in a building which is only partly open to the public is not a license or privilege to enter

or remain in that part of the building which is not open to the public. A person who enters or remains upon unimproved and apparently unused land, which is neither fenced nor otherwise enclosed in a manner designed to exclude intruders, does so with license and privilege unless notice against trespass is personally communicated to him by the owner of such land or other authorized person, or unless such notice is given by posting in a conspicuous manner. A person who enters or remains in or about a school building without written permission from someone authorized to issue such permission or without a legitimate reason which includes a relationship involving custody of or responsibility for a pupil or student enrolled in the school or without legitimate business or a purpose relating to the operation of the school does so without license and privilege.

§ 140.30 Burglary in the first degree.

A person is guilty of burglary in the first degree when he knowingly enters or remains unlawfully in a dwelling with intent to commit a crime therein, and when, in effecting entry or while in the dwelling or in immediate flight therefrom, he or another participant in the crime:

1. Is armed with explosives or a deadly weapon; or

2. Causes physical injury to any person who is not a participant in the crime; or

3. Uses or threatens the immediate use of a dangerous instrument; or

4. Displays what appears to be a pistol, revolver, rifle, shotgun, machine gun or other firearm; except that in any prosecution under this subdivision, it is an affirmative defense that such pistol, revolver, rifle, shotgun, machine gun or other firearm was not a loaded weapon from which a shot, readily capable of producing death or other serious physical injury, could be discharged. Nothing contained in this subdivision shall constitute a defense to a prosecution for, or preclude a conviction of, burglary in the second degree, burglary in the third degree or any other crime.

Burglary in the first degree is a class B felony.

§ 140.25 Burglary in the second degree.

A person is guilty of burglary in the second degree when he knowingly enters or remains unlawfully in a building with intent to commit a crime therein, and when:

1. In effecting entry or while in the building or in immediate flight therefrom, he or another participant in the crime:

(a) Is armed with explosives or a deadly weapon; or

(b) Causes physical injury to any person who is not a participant in the crime; or

(c) Uses or threatens the immediate use of a dangerous instrument; or

(d) Displays what appears to be a pistol, revolver, rifle, shotgun, machine gun or other firearm; or

2. The building is a dwelling.

Burglary in the second degree is a class C felony.

§ 140.20 Burglary in the third degree.

A person is guilty of burglary in the third degree when he knowingly enters or remains unlawfully in a building with intent to commit a crime therein.

Burglary in the third degree is a class D felony.

III. Trespass

Comment: All of the following statutes include the standard elements of trespass: (1) entering (or remaining) on the property of another, and (2) without having a legal right to be there.

§ 140.05 Trespass.

A person is guilty of trespass when he knowingly enters or remains unlawfully in or upon premises.

Trespass is a violation.

§ 140.10 Criminal trespass in the third degree.

A person is guilty of criminal trespass in the third degree when he knowingly enters or remains unlawfully in a building or upon real property

(a) which is fenced or otherwise enclosed in a manner designed to exclude intruders; or

(b) where the building is utilized as an elementary or secondary school or a children's overnight camp as defined in section one thousand three hundred ninety-two of the public health law or a summer day camp as defined in section one thousand three hundred ninety-two of the public health law in violation of conspicuously posted rules or regulations governing entry and use thereof; or

(c) located within a city with a population in excess of one million and where the building or real property is utilized as an elementary or secondary school in violation of a personally communicated request to leave the premises from a principal, custodian or other person in charge thereof; or

(d) located outside of a city with a population in excess of one million and where the building or real property is utilized as an elementary or secondary school in violation of a personally communicated request to leave the premises from a principal, custodian, school board member or trustee, or other person in charge thereof; or

(e) where the building is used as a public housing project in violation of conspicuously posted rules or regulations governing entry and use thereof; or

(f) where a building is used as a public housing project in violation of a personally communicated request to leave the premises from a housing police officer or other person in charge thereof; or

(g) where the property consists of a right-of-way or yard of a railroad or rapid transit railroad which has been designated and conspicuously posted as a no-trespass railroad zone, pursuant to section eighty-three-b of the railroad law, by the city or county in which such property is located.

Criminal trespass in the third degree is a class B misdemeanor.

§ 140.15 Criminal trespass in the second degree.

A person is guilty of criminal trespass in the second degree when he knowingly enters or remains unlawfully in a dwelling.

Criminal trespass in the second degree is a class A misdemeanor.

§ 140.17 Criminal trespass in the first degree

A person is guilty of criminal trespass in the first degree when he knowingly enters or remains unlawfully in a building, and when, in the course of committing such crime, he:

1. Possesses, or knows that another participant in the crime possesses, an explosive or a deadly weapon; or

2. Possesses a firearm, rifle or shotgun, as those terms are defined in section 265.00, and also possesses or has readily accessible a quantity of ammunition which is capable of being discharged from such firearm, rifle or shotgun; or

3. Knows that another participant in the crime possesses a firearm, rifle or shotgun under circumstances described in subdivision two.

Criminal trespass in the first degree is a class D felony.

IV. Arson

Comment: New York has five degrees of arson. Common law arson involved the burning of another person's dwelling. New York extends the crime of arson to cover other buildings and motor vehicles. The degree of arson is based on circumstances surrounding the fire and the mental state of the defendant. Circumstances that are examined include whether the fire caused endangerment to others and the method that was used by the defendant to start the fire.

§ 150.00 Arson; definitions.

As used in this article,

1. "Building", in addition to its ordinary meaning, includes any structure, vehicle or watercraft used for overnight lodging of persons, or used by persons for carrying on business therein. Where a building consists of two or more units separately secured or occupied, each unit shall not be deemed a separate building.

2. "Motor vehicle", includes every vehicle operated or driven upon a public highway which is propelled by any power other than muscular power, except (a) electrically-driven invalid chairs being operated or driven by an invalid, (b) vehicles which run only upon rails or tracks, and (c) snowmobiles as defined in article forty-seven of the vehicle and traffic law.

§ 150.20 Arson in the first degree.

1. A person is guilty of arson in the first degree when he intentionally damages a building or motor vehicle by causing an explosion or a fire and when (a) such explosion or fire is caused by an incendiary device propelled, thrown or placed inside or near such building or motor vehicle; or when such explosion or fire is caused by an explosive; or when such explosion or fire either (i) causes serious physical injury to another person other than a participant, or (ii) the explosion or fire was caused with the expectation or receipt of financial advantage or pecuniary profit by the actor; and when (b) another person who is not a participant in the crime is present in such building or motor vehicle at the time; and (c) the defendant knows that fact or the circumstances are such as to render the presence of such person therein a reasonable possibility.

2. As used in this section, "incendiary device" means a breakable container designed to explode or produce uncontained combustion upon impact, containing flammable liquid and having a wick or a similar device capable of being ignited.

Arson in the first degree is a class A-I felony.

§ 150.15 Arson in the second degree.

A person is guilty of arson in the second degree when he intentionally damages a building or motor vehicle by starting a fire, and when (a) another person who is not a participant in the crime is present in such building or motor vehicle at the time, and (b) the defendant knows that fact or the circumstances are such as to render the presence of such a person therein a reasonable possibility.

Arson in the second degree is a class B felony.

§ 150.10 Arson in the third degree.

1. A person is guilty of arson in the third degree when he intentionally damages a building or motor vehicle by starting a fire or causing an explosion.

2. In any prosecution under this section, it is an affirmative defense that (a) no person other than the defendant had a possessory or proprietary interest in the building or motor vehicle, or if other persons had such interests, all of them consented to the defendant's conduct, and (b) the defendant's sole intent was to destroy or damage the building or motor vehicle for a lawful and proper purpose, and (c) the defendant had no reasonable ground to believe that his conduct might endanger the life or safety of another person or damage another building or motor vehicle.

Arson in the third degree is a class C felony.

§ 150.05 Arson in the fourth degree.

1. A person is guilty of arson in the fourth degree when he recklessly damages a building or motor vehicle by intentionally starting a fire or causing an explosion.

2. In any prosecution under this section, it is an affirmative defense that no person other than the defendant had a possessory or proprietary interest in the building or motor vehicle.

Arson in the fourth degree is a class E felony.

§ 150.01 Arson in the fifth degree.

A person is guilty of arson in the fifth degree when he or she intentionally damages property of another without consent of the owner by intentionally starting a fire or causing an explosion.

Arson in the fifth degree is a class A misdemeanor.

V. Computer Crimes

Comments: Crimes involving computers affect a growing number of people every day. While not generally recognized, computer-related crimes touch more people, more often, than any other criminal activity. Computer viruses, Trojan-horse programs, and fraudulent emails are rampant on the Internet. Most computer users find criminal attempts to steal their money every time they check their email. Criminal statutes have been put in place to address computer related crimes. Currently, they are underused due to the cost and difficultly of identifying the criminal suspects.

§ 156.27 Computer tampering in the first degree.

A person is guilty of computer tampering in the first degree when he commits the crime of computer tampering in the fourth degree and he intentionally alters in any manner or destroys computer data or a computer program so as to cause damages in an aggregate amount exceeding fifty thousand dollars.

Computer tampering in the first degree is a class C felony.

§ 156.10 Computer trespass.

A person is guilty of computer trespass when he knowingly uses or causes to be used a computer or computer service without authorization and:

1. he does so with an intent to commit or attempt to commit or further the commission of any felony; or

2. he thereby knowingly gains access to computer material.

Computer trespass is a class E felony.

§ 156.35 Criminal possession of computer related material.

A person is guilty of criminal possession of computer related material when having no right to do so, he knowingly possesses, in any form, any copy, reproduction or duplicate of any computer data or computer program which was copied, reproduced or duplicated in violation of section 156.30 of this article, with intent to benefit himself or a person other than an owner thereof.

Criminal possession of computer related material is a class E felony.

§ 156.50 Offenses involving computers; defenses.

In any prosecution:

1. under section 156.05 or 156.10 of this article, it shall be a defense that the defendant had reasonable grounds to believe that he had authorization to use the computer;

2. under section 156.20, 156.25, 156.26 or 156.27 of this article it shall be a defense that the defendant had reasonable grounds to believe that he had the right to alter in any manner or destroy the computer data or the computer program;

3. under section 156.30 of this article it shall be a defense that the defendant had reasonable grounds to believe that he had the right to copy, reproduce or duplicate in any manner the computer data or the computer program.

§ 156.00 Offenses involving computers; definition of terms.

The following definitions are applicable to this chapter except where different meanings are expressly specified:

1. "Computer" means a device or group of devices which, by manipulation of electronic, magnetic, optical or electrochemical impulses, pursuant to a computer program, can automatically perform arithmetic, logical, storage or retrieval operations with or on computer data, and includes any connected or directly related device, equipment or facility which enables such computer to store, retrieve or communicate to or from a person, another computer or another device the results of computer operations, computer programs or computer data.

2. "Computer program" is property and means an ordered set of data representing coded instructions or statements that, when executed by computer, cause the computer to process data or direct the computer to perform one or more computer operations or both and may be in any form, including magnetic storage media, punched cards, or stored internally in the memory of the computer.

3. "Computer data" is property and means a representation of information, knowledge, facts, concepts or instructions which are being processed, or have been processed in a computer and may be in any form, including magnetic storage media, punched cards, or stored internally in the memory of the computer.

4. "Computer service" means any and all services provided by or through the facilities of any computer communication system allowing the input, output, examination, or transfer, of computer data or computer programs from one computer to another.

5. "Computer material" is property and means any computer data or computer program which:

(a) contains records of the medical history or medical treatment of an identified or readily identifiable individual or individuals. This term shall not apply to the gaining access to or duplication solely of the medical history or medical treatment records of a person by that person or by another specifically authorized by the person whose records are gained access to or duplicated; or

(b) contains records maintained by the state or any political subdivision thereof or any governmental instrumentality within the state which contains any information concerning a person, as defined in subdivision seven of section 10.00 of this chapter, which because of name, number, symbol, mark or other identifier, can be used to identify the person and which is otherwise prohibited by law from being disclosed. This term shall not apply to the gaining access to or duplication solely of records of a person by that person or by another specifically authorized by the person whose records are gained access to or duplicated; or

(c) is not and is not intended to be available to anyone other than the person or persons rightfully in possession thereof or selected persons having access thereto with his or their consent and which accords or may accord such rightful possessors an advantage over competitors or other persons who do not have knowledge or the benefit thereof.

6. "Uses a computer or computer service without authorization" means the use of a computer or computer service without the permission of, or in excess of the permission of, the owner or lessor or someone licensed or privileged by the owner or lessor after notice to that effect to the user of the computer or computer service has been given by:

(a) giving actual notice in writing or orally to the user; or

(b) prominently posting written notice adjacent to the computer being utilized by the user; or

(c) a notice that is displayed on, printed out on or announced by the computer being utilized by the user. Proof that the computer is programmed to automatically display, print or announce such notice or a notice prohibiting copying, reproduction or duplication shall be presumptive evidence that such notice was displayed, printed or announced.

7. "Felony" as used in this article means any felony defined in the laws of this state or any offense defined in the laws of any other jurisdiction for which a sentence to a term of imprisonment in excess of one year is authorized in this state.

§ 156.05 Unauthorized use of a computer.

A person is guilty of unauthorized use of a computer when he knowingly uses or causes to be used a computer or computer service without authorization and the computer utilized is equipped or programmed with any device or coding system, a function of which is to prevent the unauthorized use of said computer or computer system.

Unauthorized use of a computer is a class A misdemeanor.

§ 156.30 Unlawful duplication of computer related material.

A person is guilty of unlawful duplication of computer related material when having no right to do so, he copies, reproduces or duplicates in any manner:

1. any computer data or computer program and thereby intentionally and wrongfully deprives or appropriates from an owner thereof an economic value or benefit in excess of two thousand five hundred dollars; or

2. any computer data or computer program with an intent to commit or attempt to commit or further the commission of any felony.

Unlawful duplication of computer related material is a class E felony.

VI. Identity Theft

Comment: Identity theft or fraud occurs an estimated nine million times each year. The crime is committed when a defendant, without permission, uses the personal information of another to perform an illegal act. Typically, this information is stolen from the victim's trash or through an Internet scam.

§ 190.80 Identity theft in the first degree.

A person is guilty of identity theft in the first degree when he or she knowingly and with intent to defraud assumes the identity of another person by presenting himself or herself as that other person, or by acting as that other person or by using personal identifying information of that other person, and thereby:

1. obtains goods, money, property or services or uses credit in the name of such other person in an aggregate amount that exceeds two thousand dollars; or

2. causes financial loss to such person or to another person or persons in an aggregate amount that exceeds two thousand dollars; or

3. commits or attempts to commit a class D felony or higher level crime or acts as an accessory in the commission of a class D or higher level felony; or

4. commits the crime of identity theft in the second degree as defined in section 190.79 of this article and has been previously convicted within the last five years of identity theft in the third degree as defined in section 190.78, identity theft in the second degree as defined in section 190.79, identity theft in the first degree as defined in this section, unlawful possession of personal identification information in the third degree as defined in section 190.81, unlawful possession of personal identification information in the second degree as defined in section 190.82, unlawful possession of personal identification information in the first degree as defined in section 190.83, grand larceny in the fourth degree as defined in section 155.30, grand larceny in the third degree as defined in section 155.35, grand larceny in the second degree as defined in section 155.40 or grand larceny in the first degree as defined in section 155.42 of this chapter.

Identity theft in the first degree is a class D felony.

§ 190.79 Identity theft in the second degree.

A person is guilty of identify theft in the second degree when he or she knowingly and with intent to defraud assumes the identity of another person by presenting himself or herself as that other person, or by acting as that other person or by using personal identifying information of that other person, and thereby:

1. obtains goods, money, property or services or uses credit in the name of such other person in an aggregate amount that exceeds five hundred dollars; or

2. causes financial loss to such person or to another person or persons in an aggregate amount that exceeds five hundred dollars; or

3. commits or attempts to commit a felony or acts as an accessory to the commission of a felony; or

4. commits the crime of identity theft in the third degree as defined in section 190.78 of this article and has been previously convicted within the last five years of identity theft in the third degree as defined in section 190.78, identity theft in the second degree as defined in this section, identity theft in the first degree as defined in section 190.80, unlawful possession of personal identification information in the third degree as defined in section 190.81, unlawful possession of personal identification information in the second degree as defined in section 190.82, unlawful possession of personal identification information in the first degree as defined in section 190.83, grand larceny in the fourth degree as defined in section 155.30, grand larceny in the third degree as defined in section 155.35, grand larceny in the second degree as defined in section 155.40 or grand larceny in the first degree as defined in section 155.42 of this chapter.

Identity theft in the second degree is a class E felony.

§ 190.78 Identity theft in the third degree.

A person is guilty of identity theft in the third degree when he or she knowingly and with intent to defraud assumes the identity of another person by presenting himself or herself as that other person, or by acting as that other person or by using personal identifying information of that other person, and thereby:

1. obtains goods, money, property or services or uses credit in the name of such other person or causes financial loss to such person or to another person or persons; or

2. commits a class A misdemeanor or higher level crime.

Identity theft in the third degree is a class A misdemeanor.

§ 190.83 Unlawful possession of personal identification information in the first degree.

A person is guilty of unlawful possession of personal identification information in the first degree when he or she commits the crime of unlawful possession of personal identification information in the second degree and:

1. with intent to further the commission of identity theft in the second degree, he or she supervises more than three accomplices; or

2. he or she has been previously convicted within the last five years of identity theft in the third degree as defined in section 190.78, identity theft in the second degree as defined in section 190.79, identity theft in the first degree as defined in section 190.80, unlawful possession of personal identification information in the third degree as defined in section 190.81, unlawful possession of personal identification information in the second degree as defined in section 190.82, unlawful possession of personal identification information in the first degree as defined in this section, grand larceny in the fourth degree as defined in section 155.30, grand larceny in the third degree as defined in section 155.35, grand larceny in the second degree as defined in section 155.40 or grand larceny in the first degree as defined in section 155.42 of this chapter.

Unlawful possession of personal identification information in the first degree is a class D felony.

§ 190.82 Unlawful possession of personal identification information in the second degree.

A person is guilty of unlawful possession of personal identification information in the second degree when he or she knowingly possesses two hundred fifty or more items of personal identification information of the following nature: a person's financial services account number or code, savings account number or code, checking account number or code, brokerage account number or code, credit card account number or code, debit card number or code, automated teller machine number or code, personal identification number, mother's maiden name, computer system password, electronic signature or unique biometric data that is a fingerprint, voice print, retinal image or iris image of another person knowing such information is intended to be used in furtherance of the commission of a crime defined in this chapter.

Unlawful possession of personal identification information in the second degree is a class E felony.

§ 190.81 Unlawful possession of personal identification information in the third degree.

A person is guilty of unlawful possession of personal identification information in the third degree when he or she knowingly possesses a person's financial services account number or code, savings account number or code, checking account number or code, brokerage account number or code, credit card account number or code, debit card number or code, automated teller machine number or code, personal identification number, mother's maiden name, computer system password, electronic signature or unique biometric data that is a fingerprint, voice print, retinal image or iris image of another person knowing such information is intended to be used in furtherance of the commission of a crime defined in this chapter.

Unlawful possession of personal identification information in the third degree is a class A misdemeanor.

§ 190.84 Defenses.

In any prosecution for identity theft or unlawful possession of personal identification information pursuant to this article, it shall be an affirmative defense that the person charged with the offense

1. was under twenty-one years of age at the time of committing the offense and the person used or possessed the personal identifying or identification information of another solely for the purpose of purchasing alcohol;

2. was under eighteen years of age at the time of committing the offense and the person used or possessed the personal identifying or identification information of another solely for the purpose of purchasing tobacco products; or

3. used or possessed the personal identifying or identification information of another person solely for the purpose of misrepresenting the person's age to gain access to a place the access to which is restricted based on age.

Questions

1. While in the clothing store, Kim sees a beautiful $50 shirt that would go great with her new pair of jeans. Unfortunately, the jeans took all her money and there is not enough left to purchase the shirt. Kim decides she has to have the shirt, and she wads it up and sticks it in her purse. On her way out of the store, the alarm sounds, security guards find the shirt in Kim's purse, and she is arrested. What statutes in this chapter, if any, apply to this situation?

2. James, a hacker, hacks into the computer system at his local bank. He overcomes the bank's encryption and wires some money to a bank account he has set up in Switzerland. What statutes in this chapter, if any, apply to this situation?

3. Kelly arrives home from work to discover her TV and DVD collection are missing. There is evidence that the back door to the apartment was kicked open. Fingerprints and a confession determine that Tim is the person who took the items. What statutes in this chapter, if any, apply to this situation?

4. Hank is banned from a department store for shoplifting and is warned never to come back. A year after the warning, Hank returns to the store and attempts to buy a pair of shoes. He is recognized by the store security and police officers are called. What statutes in this chapter, if any, apply to this situation?

5. Mary breaks into her neighbor's home. She helps herself to food and drink and watches a movie on the big screen TV. When she is finished, she cleans up her mess and returns to her own home. What statutes in this chapter, if any, apply to this situation?

6. Tom purchases a box of fireworks over the Internet. He combines the gunpowder from some of the items and makes his own large exploding device. He uses the missile to damage his ex-wife's car. What statutes in this chapter, if any, apply to this situation?

7. Greg suspects his girlfriend of dating his roommate behind his back. While his roommate is out, Greg locates the roommate's email password and accesses his account. He discovers that his girlfriend is cheating on him, and he erases all of his roommate's saved emails. What statutes in this chapter, if any, apply to this situation?

8. Jill's boss fires her, and to get even she sets his car on fire. A police officer arrives before the fire department. He smashes out a window of the locked car so a fire extinguisher can be directed at the fire. The officer cuts his hand while breaking out the window. What statutes in this chapter, if any, apply to this situation?

Chapter 9
Crimes Against Public Order, Morality, and the Administration of Government

The need of the government to maintain order, morality, and a functional system of government must be balanced against the rights of the citizens guaranteed by the federal and state Constitutions. Federal, state, and local governments struggle to limit undesirable behavior, while maintaining the rights of the people they serve.

Crimes Against Public Order

I. Mob Action (Riot)

Comment: Traditionally, riots and mobs have broken out over political issues or perceived injustices. In an alarming recent development over the last ten years, the public has seen an increasing number of riots connected to sporting events. Participants in these riots face potential felony charges under the following statute.

§ 240.06 Riot in the first degree.

A person is guilty of riot in the first degree when he:

1. Simultaneously with ten or more other persons, engages in tumultuous and violent conduct and thereby intentionally or recklessly causes or creates a grave risk of causing public alarm, and in the course of and as a result of such conduct, a person other than one of the participants suffers physical injury or substantial property damage occurs; or

2. While in a correctional facility or a local correctional facility, as those terms are defined in subdivisions four and sixteen, respectively, of section two of the correction law, simultaneously with ten or more other persons, engages in tumultuous and violent conduct and thereby intentionally or recklessly causes or creates a grave risk of causing alarm within such correctional facility or local correctional facility and in the course of and as a result of such conduct, a person other than one of the participants suffers physical injury or substantial property damage occurs.

Riot in the first degree is a class E felony.

§ 240.08 Inciting to riot.

A person is guilty of inciting to riot when he urges ten or more persons to engage in tumultuous and violent conduct of a kind likely to create public alarm.

Inciting to riot is a class A misdemeanor.

§ 240.10 Unlawful assembly.

A person is guilty of unlawful assembly when he assembles with four or more other persons for the purpose of engaging or preparing to engage with them in tumultuous and violent conduct likely to cause public alarm, or when, being present at an assembly which either has or develops such purpose, he remains there with intent to advance that purpose.

Unlawful assembly is a class B misdemeanor.

§ 240.20 Disorderly conduct.

A person is guilty of disorderly conduct when, with intent to cause public inconvenience, annoyance or alarm, or recklessly creating a risk thereof:

1. He engages in fighting or in violent, tumultuous or threatening behavior; or
2. He makes unreasonable noise; or
3. In a public place, he uses abusive or obscene language, or makes an obscene gesture; or
4. Without lawful authority, he disturbs any lawful assembly or meeting of persons; or
5. He obstructs vehicular or pedestrian traffic; or
6. He congregates with other persons in a public place and refuses to comply with a lawful order of the police to disperse; or
7. He creates a hazardous or physically offensive condition by any act which serves no legitimate purpose.

Disorderly conduct is a violation.

II. Unlawful Use of Weapons

***Comment*:** Our country has a long history of private citizens arming their selves for legal and illegal reasons. Laws regulating the use of weapons date back to before the birth of the United States. New York statutes ban many types of weapons traditionally perceived as going beyond what is needed for self defense. Ballistic knives, switchblades, machine guns, sawed-off shotguns, and bombs are all examples of weapons declared to be illegal.

The carrying or possessing of a concealed weapon in your vehicle or on your person is illegal. When transporting a weapon, it must be in a nonfunctioning state or not readily accessible.

§ 265.00 Definitions.

As used in this article and in article four hundred, the following terms shall mean and include:

1. "Machine-gun" means a weapon of any description, irrespective of size, by whatever name known, loaded or unloaded, from which a number of shots or bullets may be rapidly or automatically discharged from a magazine with one continuous pull of the trigger and includes a sub-machine gun.

2. “Firearm silencer” means any instrument, attachment, weapon or appliance for causing the firing of any gun, revolver, pistol or other firearms to be silent, or intended to lessen or muffle the noise of the firing of any gun, revolver, pistol or other firearms.

3. “Firearm” means (a) any pistol or revolver; or (b) a shotgun having one or more barrels less than eighteen inches in length; or (c) a rifle having one or more barrels less than sixteen inches in length; or (d) any weapon made from a shotgun or rifle whether by alteration, modification, or otherwise if such weapon as altered, modified, or otherwise has an overall length of less than twenty-six inches; or (e) an assault weapon. For the purpose of this subdivision the length of the barrel on a shotgun or rifle shall be determined by measuring the distance between the muzzle and the face of the bolt, breech, or breechlock when closed and when the shotgun or rifle is cocked; the overall length of a weapon made from a shotgun or rifle is the distance between the extreme ends of the weapon measured along a line parallel to the center line of the bore. Firearm does not include an antique firearm.

4. “Switchblade knife” means any knife which has a blade which opens automatically by hand pressure applied to a button, spring or other device in the handle of the knife.

5. “Gravity knife” means any knife which has a blade which is released from the handle or sheath thereof by the force of gravity or the application of centrifugal force which, when released, is locked in place by means of a button, spring, lever or other device.

5-a. “Pilum ballistic knife” means any knife which has a blade which can be projected from the handle by hand pressure applied to a button, lever, spring or other device in the handle of the knife.

5-b. “Metal knuckle knife” means a weapon that, when closed, cannot function as a set of metal knuckles, nor as a knife and when open, can function as both a set of metal knuckles as well as a knife.

6. “Dispose of” means to dispose of, give, give away, lease-loan, keep for sale, offer, offer for sale, sell, transfer and otherwise dispose of.

7. “Deface” means to remove, deface, cover, alter or destroy the manufacturer’s serial number or any other distinguishing number or identification mark.

8. “Gunsmith” means any person, firm, partnership, corporation or company who engages in the business of repairing, altering, assembling, manufacturing, cleaning, polishing, engraving or trueing, or who performs any mechanical operation on, any firearm, large capacity ammunition feeding device or machine-gun.

9. “Dealer in firearms” means any person, firm, partnership, corporation or company who engages in the business of purchasing, selling, keeping for sale, loaning, leasing, or in any manner disposing of, any assault weapon, large capacity ammunition feeding device, pistol or revolver.

10. “Licensing officer” means in the city of New York the police commissioner of that city; in the county of Nassau the commissioner of police of that county; in the county of Suffolk the sheriff of that county except in the towns of Babylon, Brookhaven, Huntington, Islip and Smithtown, the commissioner of police of that county; for the purposes of section 400.01 of this chapter the superintendent of state police; and elsewhere in the state a judge or justice of a court of record having his office in the county of issuance.

11. "Rifle" means a weapon designed or redesigned, made or remade, and intended to be fired from the shoulder and designed or redesigned and made or remade to use the energy of the explosive in a fixed metallic cartridge to fire only a single projectile through a rifled bore for each single pull of the trigger.

12. "Shotgun" means a weapon designed or redesigned, made or remade, and intended to be fired from the shoulder and designed or redesigned and made or remade to use the energy of the explosive in a fixed shotgun shell to fire through a smooth bore either a number of ball shot or a single projectile for each single pull of the trigger.

13. "Cane Sword" means a cane or swagger stick having concealed within it a blade that may be used as a sword or stilletto.

14. [See also subd. 14 below] "Chuka stick" means any device designed primarily as a weapon, consisting of two or more lengths of a rigid material joined together by a thong, rope or chain in such a manner as to allow free movement of a portion of the device while held in the hand and capable of being rotated in such a manner as to inflict serious injury upon a person by striking or choking. These devices are also known as nunchakus and centrifugal force sticks.

14. [See also subd. 14 above] "Antique firearm" means:

Any unloaded muzzle loading pistol or revolver with a matchlock, flintlock, percussion cap, or similar type of ignition system, or a pistol or revolver which uses fixed cartridges which are no longer available in the ordinary channels of commercial trade.

15. "Loaded firearm" means any firearm loaded with ammunition or any firearm which is possessed by one who, at the same time, possesses a quantity of ammunition which may be used to discharge such firearm.

15-a. "Electronic dart gun" means any device designed primarily as a weapon, the purpose of which is to momentarily stun, knock out or paralyze a person by passing an electrical shock to such person by means of a dart or projectile.

15-b. "Kung Fu star" means a disc-like object with sharpened points on the circumference thereof and is designed for use primarily as a weapon to be thrown.

15-c. "Electronic stun gun" means any device designed primarily as a weapon, the purpose of which is to stun, cause mental disorientation, knock out or paralyze a person by passing a high voltage electrical shock to such person.

16. "Certified not suitable to possess a self-defense spray device, a rifle or shotgun" means that the director or physician in charge of any hospital or institution for mental illness, public or private, has certified to the superintendent of state police or to any organized police department of a county, city, town or village of this state, that a person who has been judicially adjudicated incompetent, or who has been confined to such institution for mental illness pursuant to judicial authority, is not suitable to possess a self-defense spray device, as defined in section 265.20 of this article, or a rifle or shotgun.

17. "Serious offense" means (a) any of the following offenses defined in the former penal law as in force and effect immediately prior to September first, nineteen hundred sixty-seven: illegally using, carrying or possessing a pistol or other dangerous weapon; making or possessing burglar's instruments; buying or receiving stolen property; unlawful entry of a building; aiding escape from prison; that kind of disorderly conduct defined in subdivisions six and eight of section

seven hundred twenty-two of such former penal law; violations of sections four hundred eighty-three, four hundred eighty-three-b, four hundred eighty-four-h and article one hundred six of such former penal law; that kind of criminal sexual act or rape which was designated as a misdemeanor; violation of section seventeen hundred forty-seven-d and seventeen hundred forty-seven-e of such former penal law; any violation of any provision of article thirty-three of the public health law relating to narcotic drugs which was defined as a misdemeanor by section seventeen hundred fifty-one-a of such former penal law, and any violation of any provision of article thirty-three-A of the public health law relating to depressant and stimulant drugs which was defined as a misdemeanor by section seventeen hundred forty-seven-b of such former penal law.

(b) [As amended by L.1999, c. 635, § 11. See, also, par. (b) below.] any of the following offenses defined in the penal law: illegally using, carrying or possessing a pistol or other dangerous weapon; possession of burglar's tools; criminal possession of stolen property in the third degree; escape in the third degree; jostling; fraudulent accosting; that kind of loitering defined in subdivision three of section 240.35; endangering the welfare of a child; the offenses defined in article two hundred thirty-five; issuing abortional articles; permitting prostitution; promoting prostitution in the third degree; stalking in the fourth degree; stalking in the third degree; the offenses defined in article one hundred thirty; the offenses defined in article two hundred twenty.

(b) [As amended by L.1999, c. 635, § 15. See, also, par. (b) above.] any of the following offenses defined in the penal law: illegally using, carrying or possessing a pistol or other dangerous weapon; possession of burglar's tools; criminal possession of stolen property in the third degree; escape in the third degree; jostling; fraudulent accosting; that kind of loitering defined in subdivision three of section 240.35; endangering the welfare of a child; the offenses defined in article two hundred thirty-five; issuing abortional articles; permitting prostitution; promoting prostitution in the third degree; stalking in the third degree; stalking in the fourth degree; the offenses defined in article one hundred thirty; the offenses defined in article two hundred twenty.

18. "Armor piercing ammunition" means any ammunition capable of being used in pistols or revolvers containing a projectile or projectile core, or a projectile or projectile core for use in such ammunition, that is constructed entirely (excluding the presence of traces of other substances) from one or a combination of any of the following: tungsten alloys, steel, iron, brass, bronze, beryllium copper, or uranium.

19. "Duly authorized instructor" means (a) a duly commissioned officer of the United States army, navy, marine corps or coast guard, or of the national guard of the state of New York; or (b) a duly qualified adult citizen of the United States who has been granted a certificate as an instructor in small arms practice issued by the United States army, navy or marine corps, or by the adjutant general of this state, or by the national rifle association of America, a not-for-profit corporation duly organized under the laws of this state; or (c) by a person duly qualified and designated by the department of environmental conservation under paragraph d of subdivision six of section 11-0713 of the environmental conservation law as its agent in the giving of instruction and the making of certifications of qualification in responsible hunting practices.

20. "Disguised gun" means any weapon or device capable of being concealed on the person from which a shot can be discharged through the energy of an explosive and is designed and intended to appear to be something other than a gun.

21. "Semiautomatic" means any repeating rifle, shotgun or pistol, regardless of barrel or overall length, which utilizes a portion of the energy of a firing cartridge or shell to extract the fired cartridge case or spent shell and chamber the next round, and which requires a separate pull of the trigger to fire each cartridge or shell.

22. "Assault weapon" means (a) a semiautomatic rifle that has an ability to accept a detachable magazine and has at least two of the following characteristics:

(i) a folding or telescoping stock;

(ii) a pistol grip that protrudes conspicuously beneath the action of the weapon;

(iii) a bayonet mount;

(iv) a flash suppressor or threaded barrel designed to accommodate a flash suppressor;

(v) a grenade launcher; or

(b) a semiautomatic shotgun that has at least two of the following characteristics:

(i) a folding or telescoping stock;

(ii) a pistol grip that protrudes conspicuously beneath the action of the weapon;

(iii) a fixed magazine capacity in excess of five rounds;

(iv) an ability to accept a detachable magazine; or

(c) a semiautomatic pistol that has an ability to accept a detachable magazine and has at least two of the following characteristics:

(i) an ammunition magazine that attaches to the pistol outside of the pistol grip;

(ii) a threaded barrel capable of accepting a barrel extender, flash suppressor, forward handgrip, or silencer;

(iii) a shroud that is attached to, or partially or completely encircles, the barrel and that permits the shooter to hold the firearm with the nontrigger hand without being burned;

(iv) a manufactured weight of fifty ounces or more when the pistol is unloaded;

(v) a semiautomatic version of an automatic rifle, shotgun or firearm; or

(d) any of the weapons, or functioning frames or receivers of such weapons, or copies or duplicates of such weapons, in any caliber, known as:

(i) Norinco, Mitchell, and Poly Technologies Avtomat Kalashnikovs (all models);

(ii) Action Arms Israeli Military Industries UZI and Galil;

(iii) Beretta Ar70 (SC-70);

(iv) Colt AR-15;

(v) Fabrique National FN/FAL, FN/LAR, and FNC;

(vi) SWD M-10, M-11, M-11/9, and M-12;

(vii) Steyr AUG;

(viii) INTRATEC TEC-9, TEC-DC9 and TEC-22; and

(ix) revolving cylinder shotguns, such as (or similar to) the Street Sweeper and Striker 12;

(e) provided, however, that such term does not include: (I) any rifle, shotgun or pistol that (A) is manually operated by bolt, pump, lever or slide action; (B) has been rendered permanently inoperable; or (C) is an antique firearm as defined in 18 U.S.C. 921(a)(16);

(ii) a semiautomatic rifle that cannot accept a detachable magazine that holds more than five rounds of ammunition;

(iii) a semiautomatic shotgun that cannot hold more than five rounds of ammunition in a fixed or detachable magazine;

(iv) a rifle, shotgun or pistol, or a replica or a duplicate thereof, specified in Appendix A to section 922 of 18 U.S.C. as such weapon was manufactured on October first, nineteen hundred ninety-three. The mere fact that a weapon is not listed in Appendix A shall not be construed to mean that such weapon is an assault weapon; or

(v) a semiautomatic rifle, a semiautomatic shotgun or a semiautomatic pistol or any of the weapons defined in paragraph (d) of this subdivision lawfully possessed prior to September fourteenth, nineteen hundred ninety-four.

23. "Large capacity ammunition feeding device" means a magazine, belt, drum, feed strip, or similar device, manufactured after September thirteenth, nineteen hundred ninety-four, that has a capacity of, or that can be readily restored or converted to accept, more than ten rounds of ammunition; provided, however, that such term does not include an attached tubular device designed to accept, and capable of operating only with, .22 caliber rimfire ammunition.

§ 265.04 Criminal possession of a weapon in the first degree.

A person is guilty of criminal possession of a weapon in the first degree when such person:

(1) possesses any explosive substance with intent to use the same unlawfully against the person or property of another; or

(2) possesses ten or more firearms.

Criminal possession of a weapon in the first degree is a class B felony.

§ 265.09 Criminal use of a firearm in the first degree.

(1) A person is guilty of criminal use of a firearm in the first degree when he commits any class B violent felony offense as defined in paragraph (a) of subdivision one of section 70.02 and he either:

(a) possesses a deadly weapon, if the weapon is a loaded weapon from which a shot, readily capable of producing death or other serious injury may be discharged; or

(b) displays what appears to be a pistol, revolver, rifle, shotgun, machine gun or other firearm.

Criminal use of a firearm in the first degree is a class B felony.

(2) Sentencing. Notwithstanding any other provision of law to the contrary, when a person is convicted of criminal use of a firearm in the first degree as defined in subdivision one of this section, the court shall impose an additional consecutive sentence of five years to the minimum term of an indeterminate sentence imposed on the underlying class B violent felony offense

where the person convicted of such crime displays a loaded weapon from which a shot, readily capable of producing death or other serious injury may be discharged, in furtherance of the commission of such crime, provided, however, that such additional sentence shall not be imposed if the court, having regard to the nature and circumstances of the crime and to the history and character of the defendant, finds on the record that such additional consecutive sentence would be unduly harsh and that not imposing such sentence would be consistent with the public safety and would not deprecate the seriousness of the crime. Notwithstanding any other provision of law to the contrary, the aggregate of the five year consecutive term imposed pursuant to this subdivision and the minimum term of the indeterminate sentence imposed on the underlying class B violent felony shall constitute the new aggregate minimum term of imprisonment, and a person subject to such term shall be required to serve the entire aggregate minimum term and shall not be eligible for release on parole or conditional release during such term. This subdivision shall not apply where the defendant's criminal liability for displaying a loaded weapon from which a shot, readily capable of producing death or other serious injury may be discharged, in furtherance of the commission of crime is based on the conduct of another pursuant to section 20.00 of the penal law.

§ 265.15 Presumptions of possession, unlawful intent and defacement.

1. The presence in any room, dwelling, structure or vehicle of any machine-gun is presumptive evidence of its unlawful possession by all persons occupying the place where such machine-gun is found.

2. The presence in any stolen vehicle of any weapon, instrument, appliance or substance specified in sections 265.01, 265.02, 265.03, 265.04 and 265.05 is presumptive evidence of its possession by all persons occupying such vehicle at the time such weapon, instrument, appliance or substance is found.

3. The presence in an automobile, other than a stolen one or a public omnibus, of any firearm, large capacity ammunition feeding device, defaced firearm, defaced rifle or shotgun, defaced large capacity ammunition feeding device, firearm silencer, explosive or incendiary bomb, bombshell, gravity knife, switchblade knife, pilum ballistic knife, metal knuckle knife, dagger, dirk, stiletto, billy, blackjack, metal knuckles, chuka stick, sandbag, sandclub or slungshot is presumptive evidence of its possession by all persons occupying such automobile at the time such weapon, instrument or appliance is found, except under the following circumstances: (a) if such weapon, instrument or appliance is found upon the person of one of the occupants therein; (b) if such weapon, instrument or appliance is found in an automobile which is being operated for hire by a duly licensed driver in the due, lawful and proper pursuit of his or her trade, then such presumption shall not apply to the driver; or (c) if the weapon so found is a pistol or revolver and one of the occupants, not present under duress, has in his or her possession a valid license to have and carry concealed the same.

4. The possession by any person of the substance as specified in section 265.04 is presumptive evidence of possessing such substance with intent to use the same unlawfully against the person or property of another if such person is not licensed or otherwise authorized to possess such substance. The possession by any person of any dagger, dirk, stiletto, dangerous knife or any other weapon, instrument, appliance or substance designed, made or adapted for use primarily as a weapon, is presumptive evidence of intent to use the same unlawfully against another.

5. The possession by any person of a defaced machine-gun, firearm, rifle or shotgun is presumptive evidence that such person defaced the same.

6. The possession of five or more firearms by any person is presumptive evidence that such person possessed the firearms with the intent to sell same.

Crimes Against Public Morality

I. Prostitution and Solicitation

***Comment*:** Prostitution occurs when an individual performs a physical act upon another individual for the purpose of sexual arousal or gratification in exchange for some sort of compensation. Patronizing a prostitute occurs when a person offers compensation in exchange for a sexual act.

§ 230.00 Prostitution.

A person is guilty of prostitution when such person engages or agrees or offers to engage in sexual conduct with another person in return for a fee.

Prostitution is a class B Misdemeanor.

§ 230.02 Patronizing a prostitute; definitions.

1. A person patronizes a prostitute when:

(a) Pursuant to a prior understanding, he pays a fee to another person as compensation for such person or a third person having engaged in sexual conduct with him; or

(b) He pays or agrees to pay a fee to another person pursuant to an understanding that in return therefor such person or a third person will engage in sexual conduct with him; or

(c) He solicits or requests another person to engage in sexual conduct with him in return for a fee.

2. As used in this article, "person who is patronized" means the person with whom the defendant engaged in sexual conduct or was to have engaged in sexual conduct pursuant to the understanding, or the person who was solicited or requested by the defendant to engage in sexual conduct.

II. Pandering, Pimping, and Keeping a Place of Prostitution

***Comment*:** The criminal act of compelling prostitution, or *pandering*, occurs when an individual compels another individual to become a prostitute or arranges a situation in which a person might engage in the act of prostitution. The crime of promoting prostitution, or *pimping*, occurs when someone other than a prostitute receives compensation that was earned from the act of prostitution. The compensation can be in the form of money, drugs, goods, and so forth, and cannot be payment for some type of lawful transaction. For example, a landlord who receives cash payment from a prostitute for monthly apartment rent is not guilty of pimping.

Promoting prostitution also occurs when a person arranges, or offers to arrange, a meeting with a prostitute. A violation occurs if a person directs another individual to a location where that individual can find a prostitute. For example, if a cab driver knowingly directs a passenger to a prostitute he or she would be in violation of the statute. The crime of patronizing a prostitute occurs when one uses the services of a prostitute or "remains in a place of prostitution with intent to engage in an act of sexual penetration."

The crime of permitting prostitution occurs when a person allows acts of prostitution to take place at a location that is under his or her control. To obtain a conviction, the statute requires the person to have known or at least to have had some type of forewarning that would lead a reasonable person to believe the place was being used for prostitution.

§ 230.15 Promoting prostitution; definitions of terms.

The following definitions are applicable to this article:

1. "Advance prostitution." A person "advances prostitution" when, acting other than as a prostitute or as a patron thereof, he knowingly causes or aids a person to commit or engage in prostitution, procures or solicits patrons for prostitution, provides persons or premises for prostitution purposes, operates or assists in the operation of a house of prostitution or a prostitution enterprise, or engages in any other conduct designed to institute, aid or facilitate an act or enterprise of prostitution.

2. "Profit from prostitution." A person "profits from prostitution" when, acting other than as a prostitute receiving compensation for personally rendered prostitution services, he accepts or receives money or other property pursuant to an agreement or understanding with any person whereby he participates or is to participate in the proceeds of prostitution activity.

§ 230.32 Promoting prostitution in the first degree.

A person is guilty of promoting prostitution in the first degree when he knowingly advances or profits from prostitution of a person less than eleven years old.

Promoting prostitution in the first degree is a class B felony.

§ 230.33. Compelling prostitution.

A person is guilty of compelling prostitution when, being twenty-one years of age or older, he or she knowingly advances prostitution by compelling a person less than sixteen years old, by force or intimidation, to engage in prostitution.

Compelling prostitution is a class B felony

§ 230.40 Permitting prostitution.

A person is guilty of permitting prostitution when, having possession or control of premises which he knows are being used for prostitution purposes, he fails to make reasonable effort to halt or abate such use.

Permitting prostitution is a class B misdemeanor.

III. Sexual Morals

Comment: It has long been established, although increasingly questioned, that the state has a vested interest in the sexual conduct of its citizens. Supporters of tough moral laws argue that if acts of fornication, adultery, indecency, and bigamy are left unchecked, they will undermine the social structure of our society. Critics of the laws feel the government is interfering unnecessarily in the private lives of the people.

§ 255.17 Adultery.

A person is guilty of adultery when he engages in sexual intercourse with another person at a time when he has a living spouse, or the other person has a living spouse.

Adultery is a class B misdemeanor.

§ 255.30 Adultery and incest; corroboration.

1. A person shall not be convicted of adultery or of an attempt to commit adultery solely upon the testimony of the other party to the adulterous act or attempted act, unsupported by other evidence tending to establish that the defendant attempted to engage with the other party in sexual intercourse, and that the defendant or the other party had a living spouse at the time of the adulterous act or attempted act.

2. A person shall not be convicted of incest or of an attempt to commit incest solely upon the testimony of the other party unsupported by other evidence tending to establish that the defendant married the other party, or that the defendant was a relative of the other party of a kind specified in section 255.25.

§ 255.15 Bigamy.

A person is guilty of bigamy when he contracts or purports to contract a marriage with another person at a time when he has a living spouse, or the other person has a living spouse.

Bigamy is a class E felony.

§ 245.00 Public lewdness.

A person is guilty of public lewdness when he intentionally exposes the private or intimate parts of his body in a lewd manner or commits any other lewd act (a) in a public place, or (b) in private premises under circumstances in which he may readily be observed from either a public place or from other private premises, and with intent that he be so observed.

Public lewdness is a class B misdemeanor.

§ 245.01 Exposure of a person.

A person is guilty of exposure if he appears in a public place in such a manner that the private or intimate parts of his body are unclothed or exposed. For purposes of this section, the private or intimate parts of a female person shall include that portion of the breast which is below the top of the areola. This section shall not apply to the breastfeeding of infants or to any person entertaining or performing in a play, exhibition, show or entertainment.

Exposure of a person is a violation.

Nothing in this section shall prevent the adoption by a city, town or village of a local law prohibiting exposure of a person as herein defined in a public place, at any time, whether or not such person is entertaining or performing in a play, exhibition, show or entertainment.

§ 245.02 Promoting the exposure of a person.

A person is guilty of promoting the exposure of a person when he knowingly conducts, maintains, owns, manages, operates or furnishes any public premise or place where a person in a public place appears in such a manner that the private or intimate parts of his body are unclothed or exposed. For purposes of this section, the private or intimate parts of a female person shall include that portion of the breast which is below the top of the areola. This section shall not apply to the breastfeeding of infants or to any person entertaining or performing in a play, exhibition, show or entertainment.

Promoting the exposure of a person is a violation.

Nothing in this section shall prevent the adoption by a city, town or village of a local law prohibiting the exposure of a person substantially as herein defined in a public place, at any time, whether or not such person is entertaining or performing in a play, exhibition, show or entertainment.

§ 245.05 Offensive exhibition.

A person is guilty of offensive exhibition when he knowingly produces, operates, manages or furnishes premises for, or in any way promotes or participates in, an exhibition in the nature of public entertainment or amusement in which:

1. A person competes continuously without respite for a period of more than eight consecutive hours in a dance contest, bicycle race or other contest involving physical endurance; or

2. A person is held up to ridicule or contempt by voluntarily submitting to indignities such as the throwing of balls or other articles at his head or body; or

3. A firearm is discharged or a knife, arrow or other sharp or dangerous instrument is thrown or propelled at or toward a person.

Offensive exhibition is a violation.

IV. Obscenity

***Comment*:** In regards to the crime of obscenity, New York law closely follows the guidelines set by the U.S. Supreme Court in the 1973 case of *Miller v. California*. The key to understanding obscenity is to understand its definition and how the evidence is interpreted. Obscenity is defined in statute 235.00 as material or acts that are salacious and depict, in an offensive way, sexual acts or bodily functions. The material or act must lack serious literary, artistic, political, or scientific value. The judgment of whether something is obscene may vary because the court must use "contemporary community standards" when determining if it is salacious or offensive. Contemporary community standards are much like the reasonable person standard, in that we ask: How does the average person in the community view the material?

§ 235.00 Obscenity; definitions of terms.

The following definitions are applicable to sections 235.05, 235.10 and 235.15:

1. "Obscene." Any material or performance is "obscene" if (a) the average person, applying contemporary community standards, would find that considered as a whole, its predominant appeal is to the prurient interest in sex, and (b) it depicts or describes in a patently offensive manner, actual or simulated: sexual intercourse, criminal sexual act, sexual bestiality, masturbation, sadism, masochism, excretion or lewd exhibition of the genitals, and (c) considered as a whole, it lacks serious literary, artistic, political, and scientific value. Predominant appeal shall be judged with reference to ordinary adults unless it appears from the character of the material or the circumstances of its dissemination to be designed for children or other specially susceptible audience.

2. "Material" means anything tangible which is capable of being used or adapted to arouse interest, whether through the medium of reading, observation, sound or in any other manner.

3. "Performance" means any play, motion picture, dance or other exhibition performed before an audience.

4. "Promote" means to manufacture, issue, sell, give, provide, lend, mail, deliver, transfer, transmute, publish, distribute, circulate, disseminate, present, exhibit or advertise, or to offer or agree to do the same.

5. "Wholesale promote" means to manufacture, issue, sell, provide, mail, deliver, transfer, transmute, publish, distribute, circulate, disseminate or to offer or agree to do the same for purposes of resale.

6. "Simulated" means the explicit depiction or description of any of the types of conduct set forth in clause (b) of subdivision one of this section, which creates the appearance of such conduct.

7. "Criminal sexual act" means any of the types of sexual conduct defined in subdivision two of section 130.00 provided, however, that in any prosecution under this article the marital status of the persons engaged in such conduct shall be irrelevant and shall not be considered.

§ 235.07 Obscenity in the first degree.

A person is guilty of obscenity in the first degree when, knowing its content and character, he wholesale promotes or possesses with intent to wholesale promote, any obscene material.

Obscenity in the first degree is a class D felony.

§ 235.10 Obscenity; presumptions.

1. A person who promotes or wholesale promotes obscene material, or possesses the same with intent to promote or wholesale promote it, in the course of his business is presumed to do so with knowledge of its content and character.

2. A person who possesses six or more identical or similar obscene articles is presumed to possess them with intent to promote the same.

The provisions of this section shall not apply to public libraries or association libraries as defined in subdivision two of section two hundred fifty-three of the education law, or trustees or employees of such public libraries or association libraries when acting in the course and scope of their duties or employment.

Crimes Against the Administration of Government

I. Perjury

Comment: *Perjury* is most often thought of in reference to testimony in court in front of a judge. Perjury does apply to courtroom testimony, but it also includes any situation in which an oath or affirmation is required. Court documents, such as interrogatories and proceedings in which a judge is not present such as a deposition, all require an oath or affirmation. Any false statement material to the issue in question is grounds for perjury.

§ 210.00 Perjury and related offenses; definitions of terms.

The following definitions are applicable to this article:

1. "Oath" includes an affirmation and every other mode authorized by law of attesting to the truth of that which is stated.

2. "Swear" means to state under oath.

3. "Testimony" means an oral statement made under oath in a proceeding before any court, body, agency, public servant or other person authorized by law to conduct such proceeding and to administer the oath or cause it to be administered.

4. "Oath required by law." An affidavit, deposition or other subscribed written instrument is one for which an "oath is required by law" when, absent an oath or swearing thereto, it does not or would not, according to statute or appropriate regulatory provisions, have legal efficacy in a court of law or before any public or governmental body, agency or public servant to whom it is or might be submitted.

5. "Swear falsely." A person "swears falsely" when he intentionally makes a false statement which he does not believe to be true (a) while giving testimony, or (b) under oath in a subscribed written instrument. A false swearing in a subscribed written instrument shall not be deemed complete until the instrument is delivered by its subscriber, or by someone acting in his behalf, to another person with intent that it be uttered or published as true.

6. "Attesting officer" means any notary public or other person authorized by law to administer oaths in connection with affidavits, depositions and other subscribed written instruments, and to

certify that the subscriber of such an instrument has appeared before him and has sworn to the truth of the contents thereof.

7. "Jurat" means a clause wherein an attesting officer certifies, among other matters, that the subscriber has appeared before him and sworn to the truth of the contents thereof.

§ 210.15 Perjury in the first degree.

A person is guilty of perjury in the first degree when he swears falsely and when his false statement (a) consists of testimony, and (b) is material to the action, proceeding or matter in which it is made.

Perjury in the first degree is a class D felony.

§ 210.20 Perjury; pleading and proof where inconsistent statements involved.

Where a person has made two statements under oath which are inconsistent to the degree that one of them is necessarily false, where the circumstances are such that each statement, if false, is perjuriously so, and where each statement was made within the jurisdiction of this state and within the period of the statute of limitations for the crime charged, the inability of the people to establish specifically which of the two statements is the false one does not preclude a prosecution for perjury, and such prosecution may be conducted as follows:

1. The indictment or information may set forth the two statements and, without designating either, charge that one of them is false and perjuriously made.

2. The falsity of one or the other of the two statements may be established by proof or a showing of their irreconcilable inconsistency.

3. The highest degree of perjury of which the defendant may be convicted is determined by hypothetically assuming each statement to be false and perjurious. If under such circumstances perjury of the same degree would be established by the making of each statement, the defendant may be convicted of that degree at most. If perjury of different degrees would be established by the making of the two statements, the defendant may be convicted of the lesser degree at most.

§ 210.25 Perjury; defense.

In any prosecution for perjury, it is an affirmative defense that the defendant retracted his false statement in the course of the proceeding in which it was made before such false statement substantially affected the proceeding and before it became manifest that its falsity was or would be exposed.

§ 210.30 Perjury; no defense.

It is no defense to a prosecution for perjury that:

1. The defendant was not competent to make the false statement alleged; or

2. The defendant mistakenly believed the false statement to be immaterial; or

3. The oath was administered or taken in an irregular manner or that the authority or jurisdiction of the attesting officer who administered the oath was defective, if such defect was excusable under any statute or rule of law.

§ 210.50 Perjury and related offenses; requirement of corroboration.

In any prosecution for perjury, except a prosecution based upon inconsistent statements pursuant to section 210.20, or in any prosecution for making an apparently sworn false statement, or making a punishable false written statement, falsity of a statement may not be established by the uncorroborated testimony of a single witness.

II. Bribery of a Government Agent

Comment: The crime of bribery occurs when compensation is offered with the intent to influence the performance of someone acting in an official capacity. A person accepting such a bribe is also in violation of the statute.

§ 200.04 Bribery in the first degree.

A person is guilty of bribery in the first degree when he confers, or offers or agrees to confer, any benefit upon a public servant upon an agreement or understanding that such public servant's vote, opinion, judgment, action, decision or exercise of discretion as a public servant will thereby be influenced in the investigation, arrest, detention, prosecution, or incarceration of any person for the commission or alleged commission of a class A felony defined in article two hundred twenty of the penal law or an attempt to commit any such class A felony.

Bribery in the first degree is a class B felony.

§ 200.12 Bribe receiving in the first degree.

A public servant is guilty of bribe receiving in the first degree when he solicits, accepts or agrees to accept any benefit from another person upon an agreement or understanding that his vote, opinion, judgment, action, decision or exercise of discretion as a public servant will thereby be influenced in the investigation, arrest, detention, prosecution or incarceration of any person for the commission or alleged commission of a class A felony defined in article two hundred twenty of the penal law or an attempt to commit any such class A felony.

Bribe receiving in the first degree is a class B felony.

§ 200.03 Bribery in the second degree.

A person is guilty of bribery in the second degree when he confers, or offers or agrees to confer, any benefit valued in excess of ten thousand dollars upon a public servant upon an agreement or understanding that such public servant's vote, opinion, judgment, action, decision or exercise of discretion as a public servant will thereby be influenced.

Bribery in the second degree is a class C felony.

§ 200.11 Bribe receiving in the second degree.

A public servant is guilty of bribe receiving in the second degree when he solicits, accepts or agrees to accept any benefit valued in excess of ten thousand dollars from another person upon an agreement or understanding that his vote, opinion, judgment, action, decision or exercise of discretion as a public servant will thereby be influenced.

Bribe receiving in the second degree is a class C felony.

§ 200.00 Bribery in the third degree.

A person is guilty of bribery in the third degree when he confers, or offers or agrees to confer, any benefit upon a public servant upon an agreement or understanding that such public servant's vote, opinion, judgment, action, decision or exercise of discretion as a public servant will thereby be influenced.

Bribery in the third degree is a class D felony.

§ 200.10 Bribe receiving in the third degree.

A public servant is guilty of bribe receiving in the third degree when he solicits, accepts or agrees to accept any benefit from another person upon an agreement or understanding that his vote, opinion, judgment, action, decision or exercise of discretion as a public servant will thereby be influenced.

Bribe receiving in the third degree is a class D felony.

III. Malfeasance

***Comment*:** Government officials are expected to perform their job with competence and maintain the public trust. Improper professional conduct has a negative impact, not only on those directly owed the duty but also on the rest of society.

§ 195.00 Official misconduct.

A public servant is guilty of official misconduct when, with intent to obtain a benefit or deprive another person of a benefit:

1. He commits an act relating to his office but constituting an unauthorized exercise of his official functions, knowing that such act is unauthorized; or

2. He knowingly refrains from performing a duty which is imposed upon him by law or is clearly inherent in the nature of his office.

Official misconduct is a class A misdemeanor.

§ 200.22 **Rewarding official misconduct in the first degree.**

A person is guilty of rewarding official misconduct in the first degree when he knowingly confers, or offers or agrees to confer, any benefit upon a public servant for having violated his duty as a public servant in the investigation, arrest, detention, prosecution, or incarceration of any person for the commission or alleged commission of a class A felony defined in article two hundred twenty of the penal law or the attempt to commit any such class A felony.

Rewarding official misconduct in the first degree is a class C felony.

§ 200.27 **Receiving reward for official misconduct in the first degree.**

A public servant is guilty of receiving reward for official misconduct in the first degree when he solicits, accepts or agrees to accept any benefit from another person for having violated his duty as a public servant in the investigation, arrest, detention, prosecution, or incarceration of any person for the commission or alleged commission of a class A felony defined in article two hundred twenty of the penal law or the attempt to commit any such class A felony.

Receiving reward for official misconduct in the first degree is a class C felony.

§ 200.20 **Rewarding official misconduct in the second degree.**

A person is guilty of rewarding official misconduct in the second degree when he knowingly confers, or offers or agrees to confer, any benefit upon a public servant for having violated his duty as a public servant.

Rewarding official misconduct in the second degree is a class E felony.

§ 200.25 **Receiving reward for official misconduct in the second degree.**

A public servant is guilty of receiving reward for official misconduct in the second degree when he solicits, accepts or agrees to accept any benefit from another person for having violated his duty as a public servant.

Receiving reward for official misconduct in the second degree is a class E felony.

§ 200.30 **Giving unlawful gratuities.**

A person is guilty of giving unlawful gratuities when he knowingly confers, or offers or agrees to confer, any benefit upon a public servant for having engaged in official conduct which he was required or authorized to perform, and for which he was not entitled to any special or additional compensation.

Giving unlawful gratuities is a class A misdemeanor.

§ 200.35 Receiving unlawful gratuities.

A public servant is guilty of receiving unlawful gratuities when he solicits, accepts or agrees to accept any benefit for having engaged in official conduct which he was required or authorized to perform, and for which he was not entitled to any special or additional compensation.

Receiving unlawful gratuities is a class A misdemeanor.

Questions

1. Debbie is a photographer and has opened a business website based in New York. She offers free samples of her work as a form of advertisement. There are about 20 photos on the website that are of an 18-year-old female who posed nude for her. Debbie describes the photographs as "art." The photo's are mostly full-frontal nudity and account for most of her sales. What statutes in this chapter, if any, apply to this situation?

2. Tom's son is being charged with a felony and, if convicted, could spend up to 20 years in prison. Tom does not want to see his son go to prison, so he calls the local prosecuting attorney and offers him $5,000 to dismiss the case. The prosecutor accepts his offer and the case is dismissed. What statutes in this chapter, if any, apply to this incident?

3. Bob runs an old motel in a bad part of the town in which he lives. He rents rooms by the hour to prostitutes who work in the area. What statutes in this chapter, if any, are Bob in violation of?

4. Terry was married in 1983. She soon left her husband, without obtaining a divorce, and moved to New York. Years later, she heard that her husband had been killed in a car wreck. She remarried last year, and then ran into her first husband at a high school reunion. What statutes in this chapter, if any, are Terry in violation of?

5. Phyllis carries a .38 special handgun in her purse for personal protection. Is she in violation of any of the statutes in this chapter?

6. Todd and Jane attend a baseball game. They find seats high up in the upper deck of the park. Since no one is sitting close to them, they engage in a sex act. Unknown to them, the television camera zooms in on the couple. For several seconds, their encounter is broadcast across the nation. Has there been a violation of any of the statutes within this chapter?

Chapter 10
Terrorism and Related Crimes

I. Terrorism

***Comment*:** The goal of terrorism is to cause fear among the population in an attempt to further a cause held by the perpetrator. Even threats that are not backed up by action can still have severe emotional and economic consequences. Under statute 490.20, "Making a terrorist threat," the threat must be made with the intent to intimidate or coerce the population or in an attempt to influence the government. Whether or not it is possible to carry the threat out is inconsequential.

Statute 490.25 makes it a crime to murder or kidnap another individual in an attempt to adversely affect a civilian population or influence governmental policies and conduct. If the defendant is convicted, he or she is subject to the death penalty.

§ 490.00 Legislative findings.

The devastating consequences of the recent barbaric attack on the World Trade Center and the Pentagon underscore the compelling need for legislation that is specifically designed to combat the evils of terrorism. Indeed, the bombings of American embassies in Kenya and Tanzania in 1998, the federal building in Oklahoma City in 1995, Pan Am Flight number 103 in Lockerbie in 1988, the 1997 shooting atop the Empire State Building, the 1994 murder of Ari Halberstam on the Brooklyn Bridge and the 1993 bombing of the World Trade Center, will forever serve to remind us that terrorism is a serious and deadly problem that disrupts public order and threatens individual safety both at home and around the world. Terrorism is inconsistent with civilized society and cannot be tolerated.

Although certain federal laws seek to curb the incidence of terrorism, there are no corresponding state laws that facilitate the prosecution and punishment of terrorists in state courts. Inexplicably, there is also no criminal penalty in this state for a person who solicits or raises funds for, or provides other material support or resources to, those who commit or encourage the commission of horrific and cowardly acts of terrorism. Nor do our criminal laws proscribe the making of terrorist threats or punish with appropriate severity those who hinder the prosecution of terrorists. Finally, our death penalty statute must be strengthened so that the cold-blooded execution of an individual for terrorist purposes is a capital offense.

A comprehensive state law is urgently needed to complement federal laws in the fight against terrorism and to better protect all citizens against terrorist acts. Accordingly, the legislature finds that our laws must be strengthened to ensure that terrorists, as well as those who solicit or provide financial and other support to terrorists, are prosecuted and punished in state courts with appropriate severity.

§ 490.05 Definitions.

As used in this article, the following terms shall mean and include:

1. "Act of terrorism":

(a) for purposes of this article means an act or acts constituting a specified offense as defined in subdivision three of this section for which a person may be convicted in the criminal courts of this state pursuant to article twenty of the criminal procedure law, or an act or acts constituting an offense in any other jurisdiction within or outside the territorial boundaries of the United States which contains all of the essential elements of a specified offense, that is intended to:

(i) intimidate or coerce a civilian population;

(ii) influence the policy of a unit of government by intimidation or coercion; or

(iii) affect the conduct of a unit of government by murder, assassination or kidnapping; or

(b) for purposes of subparagraph (xiii) of paragraph (a) of subdivision one of section 125.27ain of this chapter means activities that involve a violent act or acts dangerous to human life that are in violation of the criminal laws of this state and are intended to:

(i) intimidate or coerce a civilian population;

(ii) influence the policy of a unit of government by intimidation or coercion; or

(iii) affect the conduct of a unit of government by murder, assassination or kidnapping.

2. "Material support or resources" means currency or other financial securities, financial services, lodging, training, safehouses, false documentation or identification, communications equipment, facilities, weapons, lethal substances, explosives, personnel, transportation, and other physical assets, except medicine or religious materials.

3. (a) "Specified offense" for purposes of this article means a class A felony offense other than an offense as defined in article two hundred twenty, a violent felony offense as defined in section 70.02, manslaughter in the second degree as defined in section 125.15, criminal tampering in the first degree as defined in section 145.20, identity theft in the second degree as defined in section 190.79, identity theft in the first degree as defined in section 190.80, unlawful possession of personal identification information in the second degree as defined in section 190.82, unlawful possession of personal identification information in the first degree as defined in section 190.83, money laundering in support of terrorism in the fourth degree as defined in section 470.21, money laundering in support of terrorism in the third degree as defined in section 470.22, money laundering in support of terrorism in the second degree as defined in section 470.23, money laundering in support of terrorism in the first degree as defined in section 470.24 of this chapter, and includes an attempt or conspiracy to commit any such offense.

(b) Notwithstanding the provisions of paragraph (a) of this subdivision, a specified offense shall not mean an offense defined in sections 490.37, 490.40, 490.45, 490.47, 490.50, and 490.55 of this article, nor shall a specified offense mean an attempt to commit any such offense.

4. "Renders criminal assistance" for purposes of sections 490.30 and 490.35 of this article shall have the same meaning as in section 205.50 of this chapter.

5. "Biological agent" means any micro-organism, virus, infectious substance, or biological product that may be engineered as a result of biotechnology, or any naturally occurring or bioengineered component of any such micro-organism, virus, infectious substance, or biological product, capable of causing:

(a) death, disease, or other biological malfunction in a human, an animal, a plant, or another living organism;

(b) deterioration of food, water, equipment, supplies, or material of any kind; or

(c) deleterious alteration of the environment.

6. "Toxin" means the toxic material of plants, animals, micro-organisms, viruses, fungi, or infectious substances, or a recombinant molecule, whatever its origin or method of production, including:

(a) any poisonous substance or biological product that may be engineered as a result of biotechnology produced by a living organism; or

(b) any poisonous isomer or biological product, homolog, or derivative of such a substance.

7. "Delivery system" means:

(a) any apparatus, equipment, device, or means of delivery specifically designed to deliver or disseminate a biological agent, toxin, or vector; or

(b) any vector.

8. "Vector" means a living organism, or molecule, including a recombinant molecule, or biological product that may be engineered as a result of biotechnology, capable of carrying a biological agent or toxin to a host.

9. "Biological weapon" means any biological agent, toxin, vector, or delivery system or combination thereof.

10. "Chemical weapon" means the following, together or separately:

(a) a toxic chemical or its precursors;

(b) a munition or device specifically designed to cause death or other harm through the toxic properties of a toxic chemical or its precursors, which would be released as a result of the employment of such munition or device;

(c) any equipment specifically designed for use directly in connection with the employment of munitions or devices; or

(d) any device that is designed to release radiation or radioactivity at a level dangerous to human life.

11. "Precursor" means any chemical reactant that takes part at any stage in the production by whatever method of a toxic chemical, including any key component of a binary or multicomponent chemical system, and includes precursors which have been identified for application of verification measures under article VI of the convention in schedules contained in the annex on chemicals of the chemical weapons convention.

12. "Key component of a binary or multicomponent chemical system" means the precursor which plays the most important role in determining the toxic properties of the final product and reacts rapidly with other chemicals in the binary or multicomponent system.

13. "Toxic chemical" means any chemical which through its chemical action on life processes can cause death, serious physical injury or permanent harm to humans or animals, including all such chemicals, regardless of their origin or of their method of production, and regardless of

whether they are produced in facilities, in munitions or elsewhere, and includes toxic chemicals which have been identified by the commissioner of health and included on the list of toxic chemicals pursuant to subdivision twenty of section two hundred six of the public health law.

14. The terms "biological agent", "toxin", and "toxic chemical" do not include any biological agent, toxin or toxic chemical that is in its naturally occurring environment, if the biological agent, toxin or toxic chemical has not been cultivated, collected, or otherwise extracted from its natural source.

15. "Select chemical agent" shall mean a chemical weapon which has been identified in regulations promulgated pursuant to subdivision twenty of section two hundred six of the public health law.

16. "Select biological agent" shall mean a biological weapon which has been identified in regulations promulgated pursuant to subdivision twenty-one of section two hundred six of the public health law.

17. "Chemical weapons convention" and "convention" mean the convention on the prohibition of the development, production, stockpiling and use of chemical weapons and on their destruction, opened for signature on January thirteenth, nineteen hundred ninety-three.

§ 490.15 Soliciting or providing support for an act of terrorism in the first degree.

A person commits soliciting or providing support for an act of terrorism in the first degree when he or she commits the crime of soliciting or providing support for an act of terrorism in the second degree and the total value of material support or resources exceeds one thousand dollars.

Soliciting or providing support for an act of terrorism in the first degree is a class C felony.

§ 490.20 Making a terroristic threat.

1. A person is guilty of making a terroristic threat when with intent to intimidate or coerce a civilian population, influence the policy of a unit of government by intimidation or coercion, or affect the conduct of a unit of government by murder, assassination or kidnapping, he or she threatens to commit or cause to be committed a specified offense and thereby causes a reasonable expectation or fear of the imminent commission of such offense.

2. It shall be no defense to a prosecution pursuant to this section that the defendant did not have the intent or capability of committing the specified offense or that the threat was not made to a person who was a subject thereof.

Making a terroristic threat is a class D felony.

§ 490.25 Crime of terrorism.

1. A person is guilty of a crime of terrorism when, with intent to intimidate or coerce a civilian population, influence the policy of a unit of government by intimidation or coercion, or affect the conduct of a unit of government by murder, assassination or kidnapping, he or she commits a specified offense.

2. Sentencing.

(a) When a person is convicted of a crime of terrorism pursuant to this section, and the specified offense is a class B, C, D or E felony offense, the crime of terrorism shall be deemed a violent felony offense.

(b) When a person is convicted of a crime of terrorism pursuant to this section, and the specified offense is a class C, D or E felony offense, the crime of terrorism shall be deemed to be one category higher than the specified offense the defendant committed, or one category higher than the offense level applicable to the defendant's conviction for an attempt or conspiracy to commit the offense, whichever is applicable.

(c) When a person is convicted of a crime of terrorism pursuant to this section, and the specified offense is a class B felony offense, the crime of terrorism shall be deemed a class A-I felony offense and the sentence imposed upon conviction of such offense shall be in accordance with section 70.00 of this chapter.

(d) Notwithstanding any other provision of law, when a person is convicted of a crime of terrorism pursuant to this section, and the specified offense is a class A-I felony offense, the sentence upon conviction of such offense shall be life imprisonment without parole; provided, however, that nothing herein shall preclude or prevent a sentence of death when the specified offense is murder in the first degree as defined in section 125.27 of this chapter.

§ 490.35 Hindering prosecution of terrorism in the first degree.

A person is guilty of hindering prosecution of terrorism in the first degree when he or she renders criminal assistance to a person who has committed an act of terrorism that resulted in the death of a person other than one of the participants, knowing or believing that such person engaged in conduct constituting an act of terrorism.

Hindering prosecution of terrorism in the first degree is a class B felony.

§ 490.45 Criminal possession of a chemical weapon or biological weapon in the first degree.

A person is guilty of criminal possession of a chemical weapon or biological weapon in the first degree when he or she possesses:

1. any select chemical agent, with intent to use such agent to:

(a) cause serious physical injury to, or the death of, another person; and

(b) (i) intimidate or coerce a civilian population;

(ii) influence the policy of a unit of government by intimidation or coercion; or

(iii) affect the conduct of a unit of government by murder, assassination, or kidnapping.

2. any select chemical agent, with intent to use such agent to cause serious physical injury to, or the death of, more than two other persons; or

3. any select biological agent, with intent to use such agent to cause serious physical injury to, or the death of, another person.

Criminal possession of a chemical weapon or biological weapon in the first degree is a class A-I felony.

§ 490.55 Criminal use of a chemical weapon or biological weapon in the first degree.

A person is guilty of criminal use of a chemical weapon or biological weapon in the first degree when:

1. with intent to:

(a) cause serious physical injury to, or the death of, another person; and

(b) (i) intimidate or coerce a civilian population;

(ii) influence the policy of a unit of government by intimidation or coercion; or

(iii) affect the conduct of a unit of government by murder, assassination, or kidnapping;

he or she uses, deploys, releases, or causes to be used, deployed, or released any select chemical agent and thereby causes serious physical injury to, or the death of, another person who is not a participant in the crime.

2. with intent to cause serious physical injury to, or the death of, more than two persons, he or she uses, deploys, releases, or causes to be used, deployed, or released any select chemical agent and thereby causes serious physical injury to, or the death of, more than two persons who are not participants in the crime; or

3. with intent to cause serious physical injury to, or the death of, another person, he or she uses, deploys, releases, or causes to be used, deployed, or released any select biological agent and thereby causes serious physical injury to, or the death of, another person who is not a participant in the crime.

Criminal use of a chemical weapon or biological weapon in the first degree is a class A-I felony.

§ 470.24 Money laundering in support of terrorism in the first degree.

A person is guilty of money laundering in support of terrorism in the first degree when:

1. Knowing that the property involved in one or more financial transactions represents either the proceeds of an act of terrorism as defined in subdivision one of section 490.05 of this part, or a monetary instrument given, received or intended to be used to support a violation of article four hundred ninety of this part:

(a) he or she conducts one or more financial transactions which in fact involve either the proceeds of an act of terrorism as defined in subdivision one of section 490.05 of this part, or a monetary instrument given, received or intended to be used to support a violation of article four hundred ninety of this part:

(i) With intent to:

(A) promote the carrying on of specified criminal conduct; or

(B) engage in conduct constituting a felony as set forth in section eighteen hundred two, eighteen hundred three, eighteen hundred four, eighteen hundred five, eighteen hundred seven or eighteen hundred eight of the tax law; or

(ii) Knowing that the transaction or transactions in whole or in part are designed to:

(A) conceal or disguise the nature, the location, the source, the ownership or the control of the proceeds of either the proceeds of an act of terrorism as defined in subdivision one of section 490.05 of this part, or a monetary instrument given, received or intended to be used to support a violation of article four hundred ninety of this part; or

(B) avoid any transaction reporting requirement imposed by law; and

(iii) The total value of the property involved in such financial transaction or transactions exceeds seventy-five thousand dollars.

2. He or she conducts one or more financial transactions involving property represented to be either the proceeds of an act of terrorism as defined in subdivision one of section 490.05 of this part, or a monetary instrument given, received or intended to be used to support a violation of article four hundred ninety of this part:

(a) With intent to:

(i) promote the carrying on of specified criminal conduct; or

(ii) conceal or disguise the nature, the location, the source, the ownership or the control of property believed to be either the proceeds of an act of terrorism as defined in subdivision one of section 490.05 of this part, or a monetary instrument given, received or intended to be used to support a violation of article four hundred ninety of this part; or

(iii) avoid any transaction reporting requirement imposed by law; and

(b) The total represented value of the property involved in such financial transaction or transactions exceeds one hundred twenty-five thousand dollars.

Money laundering in support of terrorism in the first degree is a class B felony.

Questions

1. Hank and Mike, who are citizens of the United States, travel to another country to attend a military training camp. Both are required to swear loyalty to a religious group and take a vow to destroy anyone or any country that does not hold their beliefs. The United States considers this group to be a terrorist organization. After six weeks of training, Mike leaves to fight against the U.S. Army in Iraq. Hank returns home and begins to gather various chemicals, which he intends to use to build a poison gas bomb. He is stopped before he can assemble the weapon. What statutes, if any, have the two men violated?

2. Bob is hired by a terrorist group to murder an outspoken critic of their organization. He is not a member of the group, but agrees to the hit. After the murder, the terrorist group claims responsibility and warns others not to oppose them. What statutes in this chapter, if any, apply to this incident?

3. Shelly is the leader of an organization that wants to replace the state and federal governments with a regime that closely follows the core values that she has developed. Her followers spend time sending out mass emails to addresses gathered off the Internet. The emails describe the current governments as corrupt and encourage the people to rise up and take back their country. The emails also urge people to vote for the group's candidates. What statutes in this chapter, if any, apply to this incident?

Chapter 11
Drug Abuse and Drug Trafficking

While overshadowed by terrorism concerns, the war on drugs continues to be fought in the cities, towns, and rural communities of the United States. Each year, billions of dollars are spent in the criminal justice system in an effort to solve the substance abuse problem.

I. Cannabis (Marijuana/Marihuana)

***Comment*:** Some states have debated whether or not the possession of small amounts of marijuana should be noncriminalized. New York continues to hold persons responsible for the possession of any amount. Punishment for possession of small amounts is often a fine, but multiple convictions can be punished by up to 15 days in jail. Persons who possess more than 10 pounds of marijuana or who sell more than 16 ounces are guilty of a Class C felony.

§ 221.05 Unlawful possession of marihuana.

A person is guilty of unlawful possession of marihuana when he knowingly and unlawfully possesses marihuana.

Unlawful possession of marihuana is a violation punishable only by a fine of not more than one hundred dollars. However, where the defendant has previously been convicted of an offense defined in this article or article 220 of this chapter, committed within the three years immediately preceding such violation, it shall be punishable (a) only by a fine of not more than two hundred dollars, if the defendant was previously convicted of one such offense committed during such period, and (b) by a fine of not more than two hundred fifty dollars or a term of imprisonment not in excess of fifteen days or both, if the defendant was previously convicted of two such offenses committed during such period.

§ 221.30 Criminal possession of marihuana in the first degree.

A person is guilty of criminal possession of marihuana in the first degree when he knowingly and unlawfully possesses one or more preparations, compounds, mixtures or substances containing marihuana and the preparations, compounds, mixtures or substances are of an aggregate weight of more than ten pounds.

Criminal possession of marihuana in the first degree is a class C felony.

§ 221.55 Criminal sale of marihuana in the first degree.

A person is guilty of criminal sale of marihuana in the first degree when he knowingly and unlawfully sells one or more preparations, compounds, mixtures or substances containing marihuana and the preparations, compounds, mixtures or substances are of an aggregate weight of more than sixteen ounces.

Criminal sale of marihuana in the first degree is a class C felony.

II. Controlled Substances

Comment: Media depictions of drug busts fail to show the process that must be followed in order to legally charge a defendant with a controlled substance violation. After the drugs are recovered, a lab test must be performed to determine exactly what the substance is. Once they are identified, the substance is located in the schedules statute, section 3306 of the New York State Controlled Substances Act, which is not reproduced here due to its length. After it is determined which schedule the drug falls under, the prosecutor examines the various statutes to determine what the proper charge should be.

§ 220.00 Controlled substances; definitions.

1. "Sell" means to sell, exchange, give or dispose of to another, or to offer or agree to do the same.

2. "Unlawfully" means in violation of article thirty-three of the public health law.

3. "Ounce" means an avoirdupois ounce as applied to solids or semisolids, and a fluid ounce as applied to liquids.

4. "Pound" means an avoirdupois pound.

5. "Controlled substance" means any substance listed in schedule I, II, III, IV or V of section thirty-three hundred six of the public health law other than marihuana, but including concentrated cannabis as defined in paragraph (a) of subdivision four of section thirty-three hundred two of such law.

6. "Marihuana" means "marihuana" or "concentrated cannabis" as those terms are defined in section thirty-three hundred two of the public health law.

7. "Narcotic drug" means any controlled substance listed in schedule I(b), I(c), II(b) or II(c) other than methadone.

8. "Narcotic preparation" means any controlled substance listed in schedule III(d) or III(e).

9. "Hallucinogen" means any controlled substance listed in schedule I(d) (5), (18), (19), (20), (21) and (22).

10. "Hallucinogenic substance" means any controlled substance listed in schedule I(d) other than concentrated cannabis, lysergic acid diethylamide, or an hallucinogen.

11. "Stimulant" means any controlled substance listed in schedule I(f), II(d).

12. "Dangerous depressant" means any controlled substance listed in schedule I(e)(2), (3), II(e), III(c)(3) or IV(c)(2), (31), (32), (40).

13. "Depressant" means any controlled substance listed in schedule IV(c) except (c)(2), (31), (32), (40).

14. "School grounds" means (a) in or on or within any building, structure, athletic playing field, playground or land contained within the real property boundary line of a public or private elementary, parochial, intermediate, junior high, vocational, or high school, or (b) any area accessible to the public located within one thousand feet of the real property boundary line comprising any such school or any parked automobile or other parked vehicle located within one

thousand feet of the real property boundary line comprising any such school. For the purposes of this section an "area accessible to the public" shall mean sidewalks, streets, parking lots, parks, playgrounds, stores and restaurants.

15. "Prescription for a controlled substance" means a direction or authorization, by means of an official New York state prescription form, a written prescription form or an oral prescription, which will permit a person to lawfully obtain a controlled substance from any person authorized to dispense controlled substances.

16. For the purposes of sections 220.70, 220.71, 220.72, 220.73, 220.74, 220.75 and 220.76 of this article:

(a) "Precursor" means ephedrine, pseudoephedrine, or any salt, isomer or salt of an isomer of such substances.

(b) "Chemical reagent" means a chemical reagent that can be used in the manufacture, production or preparation of methamphetamine.

(c) "Solvent" means a solvent that can be used in the manufacture, production or preparation of methamphetamine.

(d) "Laboratory equipment" means any items, components or materials that can be used in the manufacture, preparation or production of methamphetamine.

(e) "Hazardous or dangerous material" means any substance, or combination of substances, that results from or is used in the manufacture, preparation or production of methamphetamine which, because of its quantity, concentration, or physical or chemical characteristics, poses a substantial risk to human health or safety, or a substantial danger to the environment.

§ 220.21 Criminal possession of a controlled substance in the first degree.

A person is guilty of criminal possession of a controlled substance in the first degree when he or she knowingly and unlawfully possesses:

1. one or more preparations, compounds, mixtures or substances containing a narcotic drug and said preparations, compounds, mixtures or substances are of an aggregate weight of eight ounces or more; or

2. methadone and said methadone weighs five thousand seven hundred sixty milligrams or more.

Criminal possession of a controlled substance in the first degree is a class A-I felony.

§ 220.25 Criminal possession of a controlled substance; presumption.

1. The presence of a controlled substance in an automobile, other than a public omnibus, is presumptive evidence of knowing possession thereof by each and every person in the automobile at the time such controlled substance was found; except that such presumption does not apply (a) to a duly licensed operator of an automobile who is at the time operating it for hire in the lawful and proper pursuit of his trade, or (b) to any person in the automobile if one of them, having obtained the controlled substance and not being under duress, is authorized to possess it and such controlled substance is in the same container as when he received possession thereof, or (c) when the controlled substance is concealed upon the person of one of the occupants.

2. The presence of a narcotic drug, narcotic preparation, marihuana or phencyclidine in open view in a room, other than a public place, under circumstances evincing an intent to unlawfully mix, compound, package or otherwise prepare for sale such controlled substance is presumptive evidence of knowing possession thereof by each and every person in close proximity to such controlled substance at the time such controlled substance was found; except that such presumption does not apply to any such persons if (a) one of them, having obtained such controlled substance and not being under duress, is authorized to possess it and such controlled substance is in the same container as when he received possession thereof, or (b) one of them has such controlled substance upon his person.

§ 220.43 Criminal sale of a controlled substance in the first degree.

A person is guilty of criminal sale of a controlled substance in the first degree when he knowingly and unlawfully sells:

1. one or more preparations, compounds, mixtures or substances containing a narcotic drug and the preparations, compounds, mixtures or substances are of an aggregate weight of two ounces or more; or

2. methadone and the methadone weighs two thousand eight hundred eighty milligrams or more.

Criminal sale of a controlled substance in the first degree is a class A-I felony.

§ 220.44 Criminal sale of a controlled substance in or near school grounds.

A person is guilty of criminal sale of a controlled substance in or near school grounds when he knowingly and unlawfully sells:

1. a controlled substance in violation of any one of subdivisions one through six-a of section 220.34 of this article, when such sale takes place upon school grounds; or

2. a controlled substance in violation of any one of subdivisions one through eight of section 220.39 of this article, when such sale takes place upon school grounds; or

3. a controlled substance in violation of any one of subdivisions one through six of section 220.34 of this article, when such sale takes place upon the grounds of a child day care or educational facility under circumstances evincing knowledge by the defendant that such sale is taking place upon such grounds; or

4. a controlled substance in violation of any one of subdivisions one through eight of section 220.39 of this article, when such sale takes place upon the grounds of a child day care or educational facility under circumstances evincing knowledge by the defendant that such sale is taking place upon such grounds.

5. For purposes of subdivisions three and four of this section, "the grounds of a child day care or educational facility" means (a) in or on or within any building, structure, athletic playing field, a playground or land contained within the real property boundary line of a public or private child day care center as such term is defined in paragraph (c) of subdivision one of section three hundred ninety of the social services law, or nursery, pre-kindergarten or kindergarten, or (b) any area accessible to the public located within one thousand feet of the real property boundary line comprising any such facility or any parked automobile or other parked vehicle located within one

thousand feet of the real property boundary line comprising any such facility. For the purposes of this section an "area accessible to the public" shall mean sidewalks, streets, parking lots, parks, playgrounds, stores and restaurants.

6. For the purposes of this section, a rebuttable presumption shall be established that a person has knowledge that they are within the grounds of a child day care or educational facility when notice is conspicuously posted of the presence or proximity of such facility.

Criminal sale of a controlled substance in or near school grounds is a class B felony.

III. Drug Paraphernalia

Comment: Drug paraphernalia ranges from the various devices sold at commercial "head" shops to the improvised contraptions created by the drug user.

§ 220.50 Criminally using drug paraphernalia in the second degree.

A person is guilty of criminally using drug paraphernalia in the second degree when he knowingly possesses or sells:

1. Diluents, dilutants or adulterants, including but not limited to, any of the following: quinine hydrochloride, mannitol, mannite, lactose or dextrose, adapted for the dilution of narcotic drugs or stimulants under circumstances evincing an intent to use, or under circumstances evincing knowledge that some person intends to use, the same for purposes of unlawfully mixing, compounding, or otherwise preparing any narcotic drug or stimulant; or

2. Gelatine capsules, glassine envelopes, vials, capsules or any other material suitable for the packaging of individual quantities of narcotic drugs or stimulants under circumstances evincing an intent to use, or under circumstances evincing knowledge that some person intends to use, the same for the purpose of unlawfully manufacturing, packaging or dispensing of any narcotic drug or stimulant; or

3. Scales and balances used or designed for the purpose of weighing or measuring controlled substances, under circumstances evincing an intent to use, or under circumstances evincing knowledge that some person intends to use, the same for purpose of unlawfully manufacturing, packaging or dispensing of any narcotic drug or stimulant.

Criminally using drug paraphernalia in the second degree is a class A misdemeanor.

§ 220.55 Criminally using drug paraphernalia in the first degree.

A person is guilty of criminally using drug paraphernalia in the first degree when he commits the crime of criminally using drug paraphernalia in the second degree and he has previously been convicted of criminally using drug paraphernalia in the second degree.

Criminally using drug paraphernalia in the first degree is a class D felony.

IV. Methamphetamine-related Statutes

Comment: Methamphetamine abuse is a growing problem across the United States. Problems that are associated with the drug reach every level of our society, and the negative effects reach far beyond the drug user.

§ 220.73 Unlawful manufacture of methamphetamine in the third degree.

A person is guilty of unlawful manufacture of methamphetamine in the third degree when he or she possesses at the same time and location, with intent to use, or knowing that another intends to use each such product to unlawfully manufacture, prepare or produce methamphetamine:

1. Two or more items of laboratory equipment and two or more precursors, chemical reagents or solvents in any combination; or

2. One item of laboratory equipment and three or more precursors, chemical reagents or solvents in any combination; or

3. A precursor:

(a) mixed together with a chemical reagent or solvent; or

(b) with two or more chemical reagents and/or solvents mixed together.

Unlawful manufacture of methamphetamine in the third degree is a class D felony.

§ 220.74 Unlawful manufacture of methamphetamine in the second degree.

A person is guilty of unlawful manufacture of methamphetamine in the second degree when he or she:

1. Commits the offense of unlawful manufacture of methamphetamine in the third degree as defined in section 220.73 of this article in the presence of another person under the age of sixteen, provided, however, that the actor is at least five years older than such other person under the age of sixteen; or

2. Commits the crime of unlawful manufacture of methamphetamine in the third degree as defined in section 220.73 of this article and has previously been convicted within the preceding five years of the offense of criminal possession of precursors of methamphetamine as defined in section 220.72 of this article, criminal possession of methamphetamine manufacturing material in the first degree as defined in section 220.71 of this article, unlawful disposal of methamphetamine laboratory material as defined in section 220.76 of this article, unlawful manufacture of methamphetamine in the third degree as defined in section 220.73 of this article, unlawful manufacture of methamphetamine in the second degree as defined in this section, or unlawful manufacture of methamphetamine in the first degree as defined in section 220.75 of this article.

Unlawful manufacture of methamphetamine in the second degree is a class C felony.

§ 220.75 Unlawful manufacture of methamphetamine in the first degree.

A person is guilty of unlawful manufacture of methamphetamine in the first degree when such person commits the crime of unlawful manufacture of methamphetamine in the second degree, as defined in subdivision one of section 220.74 of this article, after having previously been convicted within the preceding five years of unlawful manufacture of methamphetamine in the third degree, as defined in section 220.73, unlawful manufacture of methamphetamine in the second degree, as defined in section 220.74 of this article, or unlawful manufacture of methamphetamine in the first degree, as defined in this section.

Unlawful manufacturer of methamphetamine in the first degree is a class B felony.

VI. Money Laundering

***Comments*:** Often the greatest problem a successful criminal faces is the inability to spend his or her ill-gotten gains. Banking laws are in place, which require that an individual report all transfers of money above a certain amount. Criminals attempt to disguise the source of their profit by trying to make the money appear to be from a legitimate source. Money laundering statutes make it a crime to disguise the true source of criminal proceeds.

§ 470.00 Definitions.

The following definitions are applicable to this article.

1. "Monetary instrument" means coin and currency of the United States or of any other country; personal checks; bank checks; traveler's checks; money orders; and investment securities and negotiable instruments, in bearer form or otherwise, in such form that title thereto passes on delivery, except that "monetary instrument" shall not include payments to attorneys for legal services.

2. "Conducts" includes initiating, concluding or participating in initiating or concluding a transaction.

3. "Transaction" includes a payment, purchase, sale, loan, pledge, gift, transfer, or delivery, and with respect to a financial institution includes a deposit, withdrawal, transfer between accounts, exchange of currency, loan, extension of credit, purchase or sale of any stock, bond, certificate of deposit, or other monetary instrument, use of a safe deposit box, or any other payment, transfer, or delivery by, through, or to a financial institution, by whatever means effected, except that "transaction" shall not include payments to attorneys for legal services.

4. "Criminal conduct" means conduct which is a crime under the laws of this state or conduct committed in any other jurisdiction which is or would be a crime under the laws of this state.

5. "Specified criminal conduct" means criminal conduct committed in this state constituting a criminal act, as the term criminal act is defined in section 460.10 of this chapter, or constituting the crime of enterprise corruption, as defined in section 460.20 of this chapter, or conduct committed in any other jurisdiction which is or would be specified criminal conduct if committed in this state.

6. "Financial institution" means:

(a) an insured bank, as defined in section 3(b) of the Federal Deposit Insurance Act, 12 U.S.C. 1813(h);

(b) a commercial bank or trust company;

(c) a private banker;

(d) an agency or branch of a foreign bank in the United States;

(e) a credit union;

(f) a thrift institution;

(g) a broker or dealer registered with the Securities and Exchange Commission under the Securities and Exchange Act of 1934, U.S.C. 78a et seq.;

(h) a broker or dealer in securities or commodities;

(i) an investment banker or investment company;

(j) a currency exchange;

(k) an issuer, redeemer, or cashier of travelers' checks, checks, money orders, or similar instruments;

(l) an operator of a credit card system;

(m) an insurance company;

(n) a dealer in precious metals, stones, or jewels;

(o) a pawnbroker;

(p) a loan or finance company;

(q) a travel agency;

(r) a person licensed to engage in the business of receiving money for transmission or transmitting the same by whatever means, or any other person engaged in such business as an agent of a licensee or engaged in such business without a license;

(s) a telegraph company;

(t) a business engaged in vehicle sales, including automobile, airplane and boat sales;

(u) persons involved in real estate closings and settlements;

(v) the United States Postal Service;

(w) an agency of the United States government or of a state or local government carrying out a duty or power of a business described in this subdivision;

(x) a casino, gambling casino, or gaming establishment with an annual gaming revenue of more than a million dollars which:

(i) is licensed as a casino, gambling casino or gaming establishment under the laws of any state or any political subdivision of any state; or

(ii) is an Indian gaming operation conducted under or pursuant to the Indian Gaming Regulatory Act other than an operation which is limited to class 1 gaming as defined in subdivision six of section four of such act; or

(y) any business or agency engaged in any activity which the superintendent of banks or the United States Secretary of the Treasury determines, by regulation, to be an activity which is similar to, related to, or a substitute for activity which any business as described in this subdivision is authorized to engage.

7. "Financial transaction" means a transaction involving:

(a) the movement of funds by wire or other means; or

(b) one or more monetary instruments; or

(c) the transfer of title to any real property, vehicle, vessel or aircraft; or

(d) the use of a financial institution.

8. "Represented" means any representation made by a law enforcement officer, or by another person at the direction of, or with the approval of, such law enforcement officer.

9. "Law enforcement officer" means any public servant, federal or state, who is authorized to conduct an investigation, prosecute or make an arrest for a criminal offense.

10. For the purpose of this article, each of the five counties in the city of New York shall be considered as a separate county.

§ 470.20 Money laundering in the first degree.

A person is guilty of money laundering in the first degree when:

1. Knowing that the property involved in one or more financial transactions represents:

(a) the proceeds of the criminal sale of a controlled substance, he or she conducts one or more such financial transactions which in fact involve the proceeds of the criminal sale of a controlled substance:

(i) With intent to:

(A) promote the carrying on of specified criminal conduct; or

(B) engage in conduct constituting a felony as set forth in section eighteen hundred two, eighteen hundred three, eighteen hundred four, eighteen hundred five, eighteen hundred seven or eighteen hundred eight of the tax law; or

(ii) Knowing that the transaction or transactions in whole or in part are designed to:

(A) conceal or disguise the nature, the location, the source, the ownership or the control of the proceeds of specified criminal conduct; or

(B) avoid any transaction reporting requirement imposed by law; and

(iii) The total value of the property involved in such financial transaction or transactions exceeds five hundred thousand dollars; or

(b) the proceeds of a class A, B or C felony, or of a crime in any other jurisdiction that is or would be a class A, B or C felony under the laws of this state, he or she conducts one or more such financial transactions which in fact involve the proceeds of any such felony:

(i) With intent to:

(A) promote the carrying on of specified criminal conduct; or

(B) engage in conduct constituting a felony as set forth in section eighteen hundred two, eighteen hundred three, eighteen hundred four, eighteen hundred five, eighteen hundred seven or eighteen hundred eight of the tax law; or

(ii) Knowing that the transaction or transactions in whole or in part are designed to:

(A) conceal or disguise the nature, the location, the source, the ownership or the control of the proceeds of specified criminal conduct; or

(B) avoid any transaction reporting requirement imposed by law; and

(iii) The total value of the property involved in such financial transaction or transactions exceeds one million dollars.

2. He or she conducts one or more financial transactions involving property represented to be:

(a) the proceeds of the criminal sale of a controlled substance, or represented to be property used to conduct or facilitate the criminal sale of a controlled substance:

(i) With intent to:

(A) promote the carrying on of specified criminal conduct; or

(B) conceal or disguise the nature, the location, the source, the ownership or the control of property believed to be the proceeds of specified criminal conduct; or

(C) avoid any transaction reporting requirement imposed by law; and

(ii) The total represented value of the property involved in such financial transaction or transactions exceeds five hundred thousand dollars; or

(b) the proceeds of a class A, B or C felony or of a crime in any other jurisdiction that is or would be a class A, B or C felony under the laws of this state, or represented to be property used to conduct or facilitate such crimes:

(i) With intent to:

(A) promote the carrying on of specified criminal conduct; or

(B) conceal or disguise the nature, the location, the source, the ownership or the control of property believed to be the proceeds of specified criminal conduct; or

(C) avoid any transaction reporting requirement imposed by law; and

(ii) The total represented value of the property involved in such financial transaction or transactions exceeds one million dollars.

Money laundering in the first degree is a class B felony.

§ 470.03 Money laundering: aggregation of value; other matters.

1. For purposes of subdivisions one and three of sections 470.05, 470.10, 470.15, 470.21, 470.22 and 470.23, and for purposes of subdivisions one and two of sections 470.20 and 470.24 of this article, financial transactions may be considered together and the value of the property involved may be aggregated, provided that the transactions are all part of a single "criminal transaction" as defined in subdivision two of section 40.10 of the criminal procedure law.

2. For purposes of subdivision two of sections 470.05, 470.10, 470.15, 470.21, 470.22 and 470.23 of this article, separate occasions involving the transport, transmittal or transfer of monetary instruments may be considered together and the value of the monetary instruments involved may be aggregated, provided that the occasions are all part of a single "criminal transaction" as defined in subdivision two of section 40.10 of the criminal procedure law.

3. Nothing in sections 470.05, 470.21, 470.22, 470.23 and 470.24; paragraph (b) of subdivision one, paragraph (b) of subdivision two and paragraph (b) of subdivision three of section 470.10; paragraph (b) of subdivision one, paragraph (b) of subdivision two and paragraph (b) of subdivision three of section 470.15; or paragraph (b) of subdivision one and paragraph (b) of subdivision two of section 470.20 of this article shall make it unlawful to return funds held in escrow:

(a) as a portion of a purchase price for real property pursuant to a contract of sale; or

(b) to satisfy the tax or other lawful obligations arising out of an administrative or judicial proceeding concerning the person who provided the escrow funds.

§ 470.25 Money laundering; fines.

1. Any person convicted of a violation of section 470.05, 470.10 , 470.15, or 470.20 of this article may be sentenced to pay a fine not in excess of two times the value of the monetary instruments which are the proceeds of specified criminal activity. When a fine is imposed pursuant to this subdivision, the court shall make a finding as to the value of such monetary instrument or instruments. If the record does not contain sufficient evidence to support such a finding the court may conduct a hearing upon the issue. In imposing a fine, the court shall consider the seriousness of the conduct, whether the amount of the fine is disproportionate to the conduct in which he engaged, its impact on victims, as well as the economic circumstances of the convicted person, including the effect of the imposition of such a fine upon his immediate family.

2. The imposition of a fine pursuant to subdivision one of this section or paragraph b of subdivision one of section 80.00 of this chapter, shall preclude the imposition of any other order or judgment of forfeiture or fine based upon the same criminal conduct.

<u>Questions</u>

1. The police find 6 ounces of marijuana on Mike during a routine questioning. What crime can he be charged with?

2. Shelly makes $10,000 a month selling illegal drugs. She purchases a vending machine company in order to avoid getting into trouble with the income tax authorities. Shelly hires Fred, an accountant, to create documentation to make it appear as if the drug money is actually being earned from the vending machines. Discuss what Fred can be charged with.

3. Todd's credit card is rejected at the motel that he plans on cooking his meth at. He phones his sister and asks her if she will rent a room for him to stay in. He tells her he will pay her $200 cash once he sells his product, if she will pay for the room now. She agrees and rents the room, but she does not stay in it or participate in the actual manufacturing of the drug. What statute, if any, can be used to charge the sister?

4. Kyle is arrested for a traffic violation. When he is searched at the police station, officers find a spoon coated with a residue that tests positive for an illegal drug. The drug amount is not sufficient to charge Kyle with possession. What other violation, if any, can he be charged with?

5. While on vacation in Mexico, Charlene mails herself a package containing 12 pounds of marijuana. She is arrested when she picks up the package at the post office. What statutes, if any, is she in violation of?

6. Todd is a drug dealer from Texas. He deposits $20,000 in his sister's bank account in New York. He then asks her to buy a car for his wife to use. Has a crime been committed, and, if so, by whom?

7. Does the location that a dealer sells from have any bearing on the possible punishments she can face?

Chapter 12
Sentencing and the Criminal Law

I. Classification of Crimes for Sentencing

Comment: New York crimes are classified as *felonies*, *misdemeanors*, *violations*, and *traffic infractions*. The following New York statutes define the four types of crimes and list their classifications for purposes of sentencing.

§ 55.10 Designation of offenses.

1. Felonies.

(a) The particular classification or subclassification of each felony defined in this chapter is expressly designated in the section or article defining it.

(b) Any offense defined outside this chapter which is declared by law to be a felony without specification of the classification thereof, or for which a law outside this chapter provides a sentence to a term of imprisonment in excess of one year, shall be deemed a class E felony.

2. Misdemeanors.

(a) Each misdemeanor defined in this chapter is either a class A misdemeanor or a class B misdemeanor, as expressly designated in the section or article defining it.

(b) Any offense defined outside this chapter which is declared by law to be a misdemeanor without specification of the classification thereof or of the sentence therefor shall be deemed a class A misdemeanor.

(c) Except as provided in paragraph (b) of subdivision three, where an offense is defined outside this chapter and a sentence to a term of imprisonment in excess of fifteen days but not in excess of one year is provided in the law or ordinance defining it, such offense shall be deemed an unclassified misdemeanor.

3. Violations. Every violation defined in this chapter is expressly designated as such. Any offense defined outside this chapter which is not expressly designated a violation shall be deemed a violation if:

(a) Notwithstanding any other designation specified in the law or ordinance defining it, a sentence to a term of imprisonment which is not in excess of fifteen days is provided therein, or the only sentence provided therein is a fine; or

(b) A sentence to a term of imprisonment in excess of fifteen days is provided for such offense in a law or ordinance enacted prior to the effective date of this chapter but the offense was not a crime prior to that date.4. Traffic infraction. Notwithstanding any other provision of this section, an offense which is defined as a "traffic infraction" shall not be deemed a violation or a misdemeanor by virtue of the sentence prescribed therefor.

§ 55.05 Classifications of felonies and misdemeanors.

1. Felonies. Felonies are classified, for the purpose of sentence, into five categories as follows:

(a) Class A felonies;

(b) Class B felonies;

(c) Class C felonies;

(d) Class D felonies; and

(e) Class E felonies.

Class A felonies are subclassified, for the purpose of sentence, into two categories as follows: subclass I and subclass II, to be known as class A-I and class A-II felonies, respectively.

2. Misdemeanors. Misdemeanors are classified, for the purpose of sentence, into three categories as follows:

(a) Class A misdemeanors;

(b) Class B misdemeanors; and

(c) Unclassified misdemeanors.

Comment: After a defendant is found guilty, the court is required to impose a sentence of the type dictated by section 60.01. The actual term of years, amount of fine, and so forth are determined by the classification of the crime and the statutes contained in Penal Laws 65–85. (These sections are not reproduced here due to their extreme length.) Penal Laws 65–85 provide the means in which to calculate the possible sentence available to the court.

§ 60.01 Authorized dispositions; generally.

1. Applicability. Except as otherwise specified in this article, when the court imposes sentence upon a person convicted of an offense, the court must impose a sentence prescribed by this section.

2. Revocable dispositions.

(a) The court may impose a revocable sentence as herein specified:

(i) the court, where authorized by article sixty-five, may sentence a person to a period of probation or to a period of conditional discharge as provided in that article; or

(ii) the court, where authorized by article eighty-five, may sentence a person to a term of intermittent imprisonment as provided in that article.

(b) A revocable sentence shall be deemed a tentative one to the extent that it may be altered or revoked in accordance with the provisions of the article under which it was imposed, but for all other purposes shall be deemed to be a final judgment of conviction.

(c) In any case where the court imposes a sentence of probation, conditional discharge, or a sentence of intermittent imprisonment, it may also impose a fine authorized by article eighty.

(d) In any case where the court imposes a sentence of imprisonment not in excess of sixty days, for a misdemeanor or not in excess of six months for a felony or in the case of a sentence of intermittent imprisonment not in excess of four months, it may also impose a sentence of probation or conditional discharge provided that the term of probation or conditional discharge together with the term of imprisonment shall not exceed the term of probation or conditional discharge authorized by article sixty-five of this chapter. The sentence of imprisonment shall be a condition of and run concurrently with the sentence of probation or conditional discharge.

3. Other dispositions. When a person is not sentenced as specified in subdivision two, or when a sentence specified in subdivision two is revoked, the sentence of the court must be as follows:

(a) A term of imprisonment; or

(b) A fine authorized by article eighty, provided, however, that when the conviction is of a class B felony or of any felony defined in article two hundred twenty, the sentence shall not consist solely of a fine; or

(c) Both imprisonment and a fine; or

(d) Where authorized by section 65.20, unconditional discharge as provided in that section; or

(e) Following revocation of a sentence of conditional discharge imposed pursuant to section 65.05 of this chapter or paragraph (d) of subdivision two of this section, probation as provided in section 65.00 of this chapter or to the sentence of imprisonment and probation as provided for in paragraph (d) of subdivision two of this section.

4. In any case where a person has been sentenced to a period of probation imposed pursuant to section 65.00 of this chapter, if the part of the sentence that provides for probation is revoked, the court must sentence such person to imprisonment or to the sentence of imprisonment and probation as provided for in paragraph (d) of subdivision two of this section.

II. Death Penalty

***Comments*:** At the time of this writing, the death penalty process in the state of New York is unsettled due to procedural concerns involving due process and jury instructions. The death penalty statutes have been under attack for many years and have been overturned as unconstitutional on several occasions. The statutes in question should always be checked for validity.

The process for sentencing someone to death is set out in New York Criminal Procedure Laws section 400.27. Once convicted of first-degree murder, as per Penal Law 125.27, the court conducts a separate hearing to determine whether the defendant should be sentenced to death or to life imprisonment. The hearing is conducted using the same jury that convicted the defendant of the murder.

Aggravating and mitigating factors, as listed in Penal Law 125.27 and Criminal Procedure Law 400.27, are considered by a jury to help them determine whether or not the defendant's actions require a sentence of death. Only those aggravating factors that where proven beyond a reasonable doubt during the trial may be considered by the jury.

The jury must find that at least one aggravating factor is present or the death sentence cannot be imposed. Some of the aggravating factors to be considered include whether or not the victim was a peace officer, firefighter, or corrections worker who was performing official duties;

the killing was related to a hijacking, murder-for-hire killing, or a felony murder; the victim was testifying or participating in a criminal investigation or prosecution or giving material assistance to the state in an investigation or prosecution; the defendant is an organized crime leader who orders a killing; or the killing involved torture.

After considering the aggravating and mitigating factors, the jury must determine if the death penalty should be imposed. The jury must reach a unanimous agreement on the death sentence or the judge will sentence the defendant to imprisonment.

§ 125.27 Murder in the first degree.

A person is guilty of murder in the first degree when:

1. With intent to cause the death of another person, he causes the death of such person or of a third person; and

(a) Either:

(i) the intended victim was a police officer as defined in subdivision 34 of section 1.20 of the criminal procedure law who was at the time of the killing engaged in the course of performing his official duties, and the defendant knew or reasonably should have known that the intended victim was a police officer; or

(ii) the intended victim was a peace officer as defined in paragraph a of subdivision twenty-one, subdivision twenty-three, twenty-four or sixty-two (employees of the division for youth) of section 2.10 of the criminal procedure law who was at the time of the killing engaged in the course of performing his official duties, and the defendant knew or reasonably should have known that the intended victim was such a uniformed court officer, parole officer, probation officer, or employee of the division for youth; or

(iii) the intended victim was an employee of a state correctional institution or was an employee of a local correctional facility as defined in subdivision two of section forty of the correction law, who was at the time of the killing engaged in the course of performing his official duties, and the defendant knew or reasonably should have known that the intended victim was an employee of a state correctional institution or a local correctional facility; or

(iv) at the time of the commission of the killing, the defendant was confined in a state correctional institution or was otherwise in custody upon a sentence for the term of his natural life, or upon a sentence commuted to one of natural life, or upon a sentence for an indeterminate term the minimum of which was at least fifteen years and the maximum of which was natural life, or at the time of the commission of the killing, the defendant had escaped from such confinement or custody while serving such a sentence and had not yet been returned to such confinement or custody; or

(v) the intended victim was a witness to a crime committed on a prior occasion and the death was caused for the purpose of preventing the intended victim's testimony in any criminal action or proceeding whether or not such action or proceeding had been commenced, or the intended victim had previously testified in a criminal action or proceeding and the killing was committed for the purpose of exacting retribution for such prior testimony, or the intended victim was an immediate family member of a witness to a crime committed on a prior occasion and the killing was committed for the purpose of preventing or influencing the testimony of such witness, or the intended victim was an immediate family member of a witness who had previously testified in a criminal action or proceeding and the killing was committed for the purpose of exacting retribution upon such witness for such prior testimony. As used in this subparagraph "immediate family member" means a husband, wife, father, mother, daughter, son, brother, sister, stepparent, grandparent, stepchild or grandchild; or

(vi) the defendant committed the killing or procured commission of the killing pursuant to an agreement with a person other than the intended victim to commit the same for the receipt, or in expectation of the receipt, of anything of pecuniary value from a party to the agreement or from a person other than the intended victim acting at the direction of a party to such agreement; or

(vii) the victim was killed while the defendant was in the course of committing or attempting to commit and in furtherance of robbery, burglary in the first degree or second degree, kidnapping in the first degree, arson in the first degree or second degree, rape in the first degree, criminal sexual act in the first degree, sexual abuse in the first degree, aggravated sexual abuse in the first degree or escape in the first degree, or in the course of and furtherance of immediate flight after committing or attempting to commit any such crime or in the course of and furtherance of immediate flight after attempting to commit the crime of murder in the second degree; provided however, the victim is not a participant in one of the aforementioned crimes and, provided further that, unless the defendant's criminal liability under this subparagraph is based upon the defendant having commanded another person to cause the death of the victim or intended victim pursuant to section 20.00 of this chapter, this subparagraph shall not apply where the defendant's criminal liability is based upon the conduct of another pursuant to section 20.00 of this chapter; or

(viii) as part of the same criminal transaction, the defendant, with intent to cause serious physical injury to or the death of an additional person or persons, causes the death of an additional person or persons; provided, however, the victim is not a participant in the criminal transaction; or

(ix) prior to committing the killing, the defendant had been convicted of murder as defined in this section or section 125.25 of this article, or had been convicted in another jurisdiction of an offense which, if committed in this state, would constitute a violation of either of such sections; or

(x) the defendant acted in an especially cruel and wanton manner pursuant to a course of conduct intended to inflict and inflicting torture upon the victim prior to the victim's death. As used in this subparagraph, "torture" means the intentional and depraved infliction of extreme physical pain; "depraved" means the defendant relished the infliction of extreme physical pain upon the victim evidencing debasement or perversion or that the defendant evidenced a sense of pleasure in the infliction of extreme physical pain; or

(xi) the defendant intentionally caused the death of two or more additional persons within the state in separate criminal transactions within a period of twenty-four months when committed in a similar fashion or pursuant to a common scheme or plan; or

(xii) the intended victim was a judge as defined in subdivision twenty-three of section 1.20 of the criminal procedure law and the defendant killed such victim because such victim was, at the time of the killing, a judge; or

(xiii) the victim was killed in furtherance of an act of terrorism, as defined in paragraph (b) of subdivision one of section 490.05 of this chapter; and

(b) The defendant was more than eighteen years old at the time of the commission of the crime.

2. In any prosecution under subdivision one, it is an affirmative defense that:

(a) The defendant acted under the influence of extreme emotional disturbance for which there was a reasonable explanation or excuse, the reasonableness of which is to be determined from the viewpoint of a person in the defendant's situation under the circumstances as the defendant believed them to be. Nothing contained in this paragraph shall constitute a defense to a prosecution for, or preclude a conviction of, manslaughter in the first degree or any other crime except murder in the second degree; or

(b) The defendant's conduct consisted of causing or aiding, without the use of duress or deception, another person to commit suicide. Nothing contained in this paragraph shall constitute a defense to a prosecution for, or preclude a conviction of, manslaughter in the second degree or any other crime except murder in the second degree.

Murder in the first degree is a class A-I felony.

§ 400.27 Procedure for determining sentence upon conviction for the offense of murder in the first degree.

1. Upon the conviction of a defendant for the offense of murder in the first degree as defined by section 125.27 of the penal law, the court shall promptly conduct a separate sentencing proceeding to determine whether the defendant shall be sentenced to death or to life imprisonment without parole pursuant to subdivision five of section 70.00 of the penal law. Nothing in this section shall be deemed to preclude the people at any time from determining that the death penalty shall not be sought in a particular case, in which case the separate sentencing proceeding shall not be conducted and the court may sentence such defendant to life imprisonment without parole or to a sentence of imprisonment for the class A-I felony of murder in the first degree other than a sentence of life imprisonment without parole.

2. The separate sentencing proceeding provided for by this section shall be conducted before the court sitting with the jury that found the defendant guilty. The court may discharge the jury and impanel another jury only in extraordinary circumstances and upon a showing of good cause, which may include, but is not limited to, a finding of prejudice to either party. If a new jury is impaneled, it shall be formed in accordance with the procedures in article two hundred seventy of this chapter. Before proceeding with the jury that found the defendant guilty, the court shall determine whether any juror has a state of mind that is likely to preclude the juror from rendering an impartial decision based upon the evidence adduced during the proceeding. In making such determination the court shall personally examine each juror individually outside the presence of the other jurors. The scope of the examination shall be within the discretion of the court and may include questions supplied by the parties as the court deems proper. The proceedings provided for in this subdivision shall be conducted on the record; provided, however, that upon motion of either party, and for good cause shown, the court may direct that all or a portion of the record of such proceedings be sealed. In the event the court determines that a juror has such a state of mind, the court shall discharge the juror and replace the juror with the alternate juror whose name was first drawn and called. If no alternate juror is available, the court must discharge the jury and impanel another jury in accordance with article two hundred seventy of this chapter.

3. For the purposes of a proceeding under this section each subparagraph of paragraph (a) of subdivision one of section 125.27 of the penal law shall be deemed to define an aggravating factor. Except as provided in subdivision seven of this section, at a sentencing proceeding pursuant to this section the only aggravating factors that the jury may consider are those proven beyond a reasonable doubt at trial, and no other aggravating factors may be considered. Whether a sentencing proceeding is conducted before the jury that found the defendant guilty or before another jury, the aggravating factor or factors proved at trial shall be deemed established beyond a reasonable doubt at the separate sentencing proceeding and shall not be relitigated. Where the jury is to determine sentences for concurrent counts of murder in the first degree, the aggravating factor included in each count shall be deemed to be an aggravating factor for the purpose of the jury's consideration in determining the sentence to be imposed on each such count.

4. The court on its own motion or on motion of either party, in the interest of justice or to avoid prejudice to either party, may delay the commencement of the separate sentencing proceeding.

5. Notwithstanding the provisions of article three hundred ninety of this chapter, where a defendant is found guilty of murder in the first degree, no presentence investigation shall be conducted; provided, however, that where the court is to impose a sentence of imprisonment, a presentence investigation shall be conducted and a presentence report shall be prepared in accordance with the provisions of such article.

6. At the sentencing proceeding the people shall not relitigate the existence of aggravating factors proved at the trial or otherwise present evidence, except, subject to the rules governing admission of evidence in the trial of a criminal action, in rebuttal of the defendant's evidence. However, when the sentencing proceeding is conducted before a newly impaneled jury, the people may present evidence to the extent reasonably necessary to inform the jury of the nature and circumstances of the count or counts of murder in the first degree for which the defendant was convicted in sufficient detail to permit the jury to determine the weight to be accorded the aggravating factor or factors established at trial. Whenever the people present such evidence, the court must instruct the jury in its charge that any facts elicited by the people that are not essential to the verdict of guilty on such count or counts shall not be deemed established beyond a reasonable doubt. Subject to the rules governing the admission of evidence in the trial of a criminal action, the defendant may present any evidence relevant to any mitigating factor set forth in subdivision nine of this section; provided, however, the defendant shall not be precluded from the admission of reliable hearsay evidence. The burden of establishing any of the mitigating factors set forth in subdivision nine of this section shall be on the defendant, and must be proven by a preponderance of the evidence. The people shall not offer evidence or argument relating to any mitigating factor except in rebuttal of evidence offered by the defendant.

7. (a) The people may present evidence at the sentencing proceeding to prove that in the ten year period prior to the commission of the crime of murder in the first degree for which the defendant was convicted, the defendant has previously been convicted of two or more offenses committed on different occasions; provided, that each such offense shall be either (i) a class A felony offense other than one defined in article two hundred twenty of the penal law, a class B violent felony offense specified in paragraph (a) of subdivision one of section 70.02 of the penal law, or a felony offense under the penal law a necessary element of which involves either the use or attempted use or threatened use of a deadly weapon or the intentional infliction of or the attempted intentional infliction of serious physical injury or death, or (ii) an offense under the

laws of another state or of the United States punishable by a term of imprisonment of more than one year a necessary element of which involves either the use or attempted use or threatened use of a deadly weapon or the intentional infliction of or the attempted intentional infliction of serious physical injury or death. For the purpose of this paragraph, the term "deadly weapon" shall have the meaning set forth in subdivision twelve of section 10.00 of the penal law. In calculating the ten year period under this paragraph, any period of time during which the defendant was incarcerated for any reason between the time of commission of any of the prior felony offenses and the time of commission of the crime of murder in the first degree shall be excluded and such ten year period shall be extended by a period or periods equal to the time served under such incarceration. The defendant's conviction of two or more such offenses shall, if proven at the sentencing proceeding, constitute an aggravating factor.

(b) In order to be deemed established, an aggravating factor set forth in this subdivision must be proven by the people beyond a reasonable doubt and the jury must unanimously find such factor to have been so proven. The defendant may present evidence relating to an aggravating factor defined in this subdivision and either party may offer evidence in rebuttal. Any evidence presented by either party relating to such factor shall be subject to the rules governing admission of evidence in the trial of a criminal action.

(c) Whenever the people intend to offer evidence of an aggravating factor set forth in this subdivision, the people must within a reasonable time prior to trial file with the court and serve upon the defendant a notice of intention to offer such evidence. Whenever the people intend to offer evidence of the aggravating factor set forth in paragraph (a) of this subdivision, the people shall file with the notice of intention to offer such evidence a statement setting forth the date and place of each of the alleged offenses in paragraph (a) of this subdivision. The provisions of section 400.15 of this chapter, except for subdivisions one and two thereof, shall be followed.

8. Consistent with the provisions of this section, the people and the defendant shall be given fair opportunity to rebut any evidence received at the separate sentencing proceeding.

9. Mitigating factors shall include the following:

(a) The defendant has no significant history of prior criminal convictions involving the use of violence against another person;

(b) The defendant was mentally retarded at the time of the crime, or the defendant's mental capacity was impaired or his ability to conform his conduct to the requirements of law was impaired but not so impaired in either case as to constitute a defense to prosecution;

(c) The defendant was under duress or under the domination of another person, although not such duress or domination as to constitute a defense to prosecution;

(d) The defendant was criminally liable for the present offense of murder committed by another, but his participation in the offense was relatively minor although not so minor as to constitute a defense to prosecution;

(e) The murder was committed while the defendant was mentally or emotionally disturbed or under the influence of alcohol or any drug, although not to such an extent as to constitute a defense to prosecution; or

(f) Any other circumstance concerning the crime, the defendant's state of mind or condition at the time of the crime, or the defendant's character, background or record that would be relevant to mitigation or punishment for the crime.

10. At the conclusion of all the evidence, the people and the defendant may present argument in summation for or against the sentence sought by the people. The people may deliver the first summation and the defendant may then deliver the last summation. Thereafter, the court shall deliver a charge to the jury on any matters appropriate in the circumstances. In its charge, the court must instruct the jury that with respect to each count of murder in the first degree the jury should consider whether or not a sentence of death should be imposed and whether or not a sentence of life imprisonment without parole should be imposed, and that the jury must be unanimous with respect to either sentence. The court must also instruct the jury that in the event the jury fails to reach unanimous agreement with respect to the sentence, the court will sentence the defendant to a term of imprisonment with a minimum term of between twenty and twenty-five years and a maximum term of life. Following the court's charge, the jury shall retire to consider the sentence to be imposed. Unless inconsistent with the provisions of this section, the provisions of sections 310.10, 310.20 and 310.30 shall govern the deliberations of the jury.

11. (a) The jury may not direct imposition of a sentence of death unless it unanimously finds beyond a reasonable doubt that the aggravating factor or factors substantially outweigh the mitigating factor or factors established, if any, and unanimously determines that the penalty of death should be imposed. Any member or members of the jury who find a mitigating factor to have been proven by the defendant by a preponderance of the evidence may consider such factor established regardless of the number of jurors who concur that the factor has been established.

(b) If the jury directs imposition of either a sentence of death or life imprisonment without parole, it shall specify on the record those mitigating and aggravating factors considered and those mitigating factors established by the defendant, if any.

(c) With respect to a count or concurrent counts of murder in the first degree, the court may direct the jury to cease deliberation with respect to the sentence or sentences to be imposed if the jury has deliberated for an extensive period of time without reaching unanimous agreement on the sentence or sentences to be imposed and the court is satisfied that any such agreement is unlikely within a reasonable time. The provisions of this paragraph shall apply with respect to consecutive counts of murder in the first degree. In the event the jury is unable to reach unanimous agreement, the court must sentence the defendant in accordance with subdivisions one through three of section 70.00 of the penal law with respect to any count or counts of murder in the first degree upon which the jury failed to reach unanimous agreement as to the sentence to be imposed.

(d) If the jury unanimously determines that a sentence of death should be imposed, the court must thereupon impose a sentence of death. Thereafter, however, the court may, upon written motion of the defendant, set aside the sentence of death upon any of the grounds set forth in section 330.30. The procedures set forth in sections 330.40 and 330.50, as applied to separate sentencing proceedings under this section, shall govern the motion and the court upon granting the motion shall, except as may otherwise be required by subdivision one of section 330.50, direct a new sentencing proceeding pursuant to this section. Upon granting the motion upon any of the grounds set forth in section 330.30 and setting aside the sentence, the court must afford the people a reasonable period of time, which shall not be less than ten days, to determine whether to take an appeal from the order setting aside the sentence of death. The taking of an appeal by the people stays the effectiveness of that portion of the court's order that directs a new sentencing proceeding.

(e) If the jury unanimously determines that a sentence of life imprisonment without parole should be imposed the court must thereupon impose a sentence of life imprisonment without parole.

(f) Where a sentence has been unanimously determined by the jury it must be recorded on the minutes and read to the jury, and the jurors must be collectively asked whether such is their sentence. Even though no juror makes any declaration in the negative, the jury must, if either party makes such an application, be polled and each juror separately asked whether the sentence announced by the foreman is in all respects his or her sentence. If, upon either the collective or the separate inquiry, any juror answers in the negative, the court must refuse to accept the sentence and must direct the jury to resume its deliberation. If no disagreement is expressed, the jury must be discharged from the case.

12. (a) Upon the conviction of a defendant for the offense of murder in the first degree as defined in section 125.27 of the penal law, the court shall, upon oral or written motion of the defendant based upon a showing that there is reasonable cause to believe that the defendant is mentally retarded, promptly conduct a hearing without a jury to determine whether the defendant is mentally retarded. Upon the consent of both parties, such a hearing, or a portion thereof, may be conducted by the court contemporaneously with the separate sentencing proceeding in the presence of the sentencing jury, which in no event shall be the trier of fact with respect to the hearing. At such hearing the defendant has the burden of proof by a preponderance of the evidence that he or she is mentally retarded. The court shall defer rendering any finding pursuant to this subdivision as to whether the defendant is mentally retarded until a sentence is imposed pursuant to this section.

(b) In the event the defendant is sentenced pursuant to this section to life imprisonment without parole or to a term of imprisonment for the class A-I felony of murder in the first degree other than a sentence of life imprisonment without parole, the court shall not render a finding with respect to whether the defendant is mentally retarded.

(c) In the event the defendant is sentenced pursuant to this section to death, the court shall thereupon render a finding with respect to whether the defendant is mentally retarded. If the court finds the defendant is mentally retarded, the court shall set aside the sentence of death and sentence the defendant either to life imprisonment without parole or to a term of imprisonment for the class A-I felony of murder in the first degree other than a sentence of life imprisonment without parole. If the court finds the defendant is not mentally retarded, then such sentence of death shall not be set aside pursuant to this subdivision.

(d) In the event that a defendant is convicted of murder in the first degree pursuant to subparagraph (iii) of paragraph (a) of subdivision one of section 125.27 of the penal law, and the killing occurred while the defendant was confined or under custody in a state correctional facility or local correctional institution, and a sentence of death is imposed, such sentence may not be set aside pursuant to this subdivision upon the ground that the defendant is mentally retarded. Nothing in this paragraph or paragraph (a) of this subdivision shall preclude a defendant from presenting mitigating evidence of mental retardation at the separate sentencing proceeding.

(e) The foregoing provisions of this subdivision notwithstanding, at a reasonable time prior to the commencement of trial the defendant may, upon a written motion alleging reasonable cause to believe the defendant is mentally retarded, apply for an order directing that a mental retardation hearing be conducted prior to trial. If, upon review of the defendant's motion and any response thereto, the court finds reasonable cause to believe the defendant is mentally retarded, it shall promptly conduct a hearing without a jury to determine whether the defendant is mentally retarded. In the event the court finds after the hearing that the defendant is not mentally retarded, the court must, prior to commencement of trial, enter an order so stating, but nothing in this paragraph shall preclude a defendant from presenting mitigating evidence of mental retardation at a separate sentencing proceeding. In the event the court finds after the hearing that the defendant, based upon a preponderance of the evidence, is mentally retarded, the court must, prior to commencement of trial, enter an order so stating. Unless the order is reversed on an appeal by the people or unless the provisions of paragraph (d) of this subdivision apply, a separate sentencing proceeding under this section shall not be conducted if the defendant is thereafter convicted of murder in the first degree. In the event a separate sentencing proceeding is not conducted, the court, upon conviction of a defendant for the crime of murder in the first degree, shall sentence the defendant to life imprisonment without parole or to a sentence of imprisonment for the class A-I felony of murder in the first degree other than a sentence of life imprisonment without parole. Whenever a mental retardation hearing is held and a finding is rendered pursuant to this paragraph, the court may not conduct a hearing pursuant to paragraph (a) of this subdivision. For purposes of this subdivision and paragraph (b) of subdivision nine of this section, "mental retardation" means significantly subaverage general intellectual functioning existing concurrently with deficits in adaptive behavior which were manifested before the age of eighteen.

(f) In the event the court enters an order pursuant to paragraph (e) of this subdivision finding that the defendant is mentally retarded, the people may appeal as of right from the order pursuant to subdivision ten of section 450.20 of this chapter. Upon entering such an order the court must afford the people a reasonable period of time, which shall not be less than ten days, to determine whether to take an appeal from the order finding that the defendant is mentally retarded. The taking of an appeal by the people stays the effectiveness of the court's order and any order fixing a date for trial. Within six months of the effective date of this subdivision, the court of appeals shall adopt rules to ensure that appeals pursuant to this paragraph are expeditiously perfected, reviewed and determined so that pretrial delays are minimized. Prior to adoption of the rules, the court of appeals shall issue proposed rules and receive written comments thereon from interested parties.

13. (a) As used in this subdivision, the term "psychiatric evidence" means evidence of mental disease, defect or condition in connection with either a mitigating factor defined in this section or a mental retardation hearing pursuant to this section to be offered by a psychiatrist, psychologist or other person who has received training, or education, or has experience relating to the identification, diagnosis, treatment or evaluation of mental disease, mental defect or mental condition.

(b) When either party intends to offer psychiatric evidence, the party must, within a reasonable time prior to trial, serve upon the other party and file with the court a written notice of intention to present psychiatric evidence. The notice shall include a brief but detailed statement specifying the witness, nature and type of psychiatric evidence sought to be introduced. If either party fails to serve and file written notice, no psychiatric evidence is admissible unless the party failing to file thereafter serves and files such notice and the court affords the other party an adjournment for a reasonable period. If a party fails to give timely notice, the court in its discretion may impose upon offending counsel a reasonable monetary sanction for an intentional failure but may not in any event preclude the psychiatric evidence. In the event a monetary sanction is imposed, the offending counsel shall be personally liable therefor, and shall not receive reimbursement of any kind from any source in order to pay the cost of such monetary sanction. Nothing contained herein shall preclude the court from entering an order directing a party to provide timely notice.

(c) When a defendant serves notice pursuant to this subdivision, the district attorney may make application, upon notice to the defendant, for an order directing that the defendant submit to an examination by a psychiatrist, licensed psychologist, or licensed clinical social worker designated by the district attorney, for the purpose of rebutting evidence offered by the defendant with respect to a mental disease, defect, or condition in connection with either a mitigating factor defined in this section, including whether the defendant was acting under duress, was mentally or emotionally disturbed or mentally retarded, or was under the influence of alcohol or any drug. If the application is granted, the district attorney shall schedule a time and place for the examination, which shall be recorded. Counsel for the people and the defendant shall have the right to be present at the examination. A transcript of the examination shall be made available to the defendant and the district attorney promptly after its conclusion. The district attorney shall promptly serve on the defendant a written copy of the findings and evaluation of the examiner. If the court finds that the defendant has wilfully refused to cooperate fully in an examination pursuant to this paragraph, it shall, upon request of the district attorney, instruct the jury that the defendant did not submit to or cooperate fully in such psychiatric examination. When a defendant is subjected to an examination pursuant to an order issued in accordance with this subdivision, any statement made by the defendant for the purpose of the examination shall be inadmissible in evidence against him in any criminal action or proceeding on any issue other than that of whether a mitigating factor has been established or whether the defendant is mentally retarded, but such statement is admissible upon such an issue whether or not it would otherwise be deemed a privileged communication.

14. (a) At a reasonable time prior to the sentencing proceeding or a mental retardation hearing:

(i) the prosecutor shall, unless previously disclosed and subject to a protective order, make available to the defendant the statements and information specified in subdivision one of section 240.45 and make available for inspection, photographing, copying or testing the property specified in subdivision one of section 240.20; and

(ii) the defendant shall, unless previously disclosed and subject to a protective order, make available to the prosecution the statements and information specified in subdivision two of section 240.45 and make available for inspection, photographing, copying or testing, subject to constitutional limitations, the reports, documents and other property specified in subdivision one of section 240.30.

(b) Where a party refuses to make disclosure pursuant to this section, the provisions of section 240.35, subdivision one of section 240.40 and section 240.50 shall apply.

(c) If, after complying with the provisions of this section or an order pursuant thereto, a party finds either before or during a sentencing proceeding or mental retardation hearing, additional material subject to discovery or covered by court order, the party shall promptly make disclosure or apply for a protective order.

(d) If the court finds that a party has failed to comply with any of the provisions of this section, the court may enter any of the orders specified in subdivision one of section 240.70.

15. The court of appeals shall formulate and adopt rules for the development of forms for use by the jury in recording its findings and determinations of sentence.

III. Special Death Sentence Considerations

***Comment*:** New York Correction Law Article 22-B—The Death Penalty establishes the procedures to follow when dealing with special circumstances, such as when a defendant is pregnant or mentally incompetent.

§ 656.00 Proceeding when person under sentence of death may be incompetent.

1. The state may not execute an inmate who is incompetent. An inmate is "incompetent" when, as a result of mental disease or defect, he lacks the mental capacity to understand the nature and effect of the death penalty and why it is to be carried out.

2. Upon the filing of a petition in the supreme court in either the county in which an inmate sentenced to death is confined or in the county in which the inmate was prosecuted alleging that the inmate is incompetent, the court shall issue an order staying the execution if and to the extent a stay is necessary to permit determination of the petition. Upon application of either the inmate's counsel or the district attorney the petition may be transferred to the court in which the inmate was convicted unless such transfer would be unduly burdensome or impracticable. Promptly upon filing the petition, the court shall appoint a commission of three psychiatric examiners, hereinafter referred to as "the psychiatric commissioners," to inquire into the inmate's competence and report to the court as to the inmate's competence. The psychiatric commissioners shall be impartial and must be qualified psychiatrists or certified psychologists. Before commencing an inquiry, the psychiatric commissioners must take the oath prescribed in rule forty-three hundred fifteen of the civil practice law and rules to be taken by referees. The petition may be filed by the inmate, the inmate's counsel, an employee of the department, the inmate's legal guardian, a member of such inmate's immediate family or, in the event that the inmate does not have regular contact with a member of his or her immediate family, a bona fide friend who has maintained regular contact with the inmate. The petition must be accompanied by an affidavit of at least one qualified psychiatrist or certified psychologist who, based at least in part on personal examination, attests that in the psychiatrist's or psychologist's professional opinion the inmate is incompetent and lists the pertinent facts therefor. For purposes of this section the terms "qualified psychiatrist" and "certified psychologist" have the meaning set forth in section 730.10 of the criminal procedure law.

3. The petition shall be served upon either the district attorney who prosecuted the inmate or upon the district attorney for the county in which the inmate is confined. If the petition is served upon the district attorney for the county in which the inmate is confined, the court shall promptly notify the district attorney who prosecuted the inmate. Immediately upon appointing the psychiatric commissioners, the court shall direct that an examination of the convicted person

promptly take place with all three of the psychiatric commissioners present at the same time. The court shall also direct, upon application of the inmate or the district attorney, that the inmate be examined by a qualified psychiatrist or certified psychologist designated by the inmate or the district attorney. Counsel for the inmate and the district attorney shall have the right to be present at each such examination. Upon the filing of a petition pursuant to subdivision two of this section, if the inmate does not have counsel and is financially unable to obtain counsel the court shall appoint competent counsel experienced in the trial of criminal matters to represent the inmate.

4. The psychiatric commissioners must receive and consider evidence offered by the inmate's counsel and the district attorney, including written submissions, testimony and expert psychiatric evidence. The proceeding before the psychiatric commissioners shall be conducted on the record but need not be conducted in accordance with the rules governing the admission of evidence at trial, but counsel for the people and the inmate shall have the right to cross-examine witnesses.

5. When the proceeding before the psychiatric commissioners has been concluded, they must forthwith provide a transcript of the proceeding, together with their findings of fact, to the court with their opinion thereon. Unless impracticable, the psychiatric commissioners shall so act within sixty days from the filing of the petition. When an inmate shall be found incompetent by a majority of the psychiatric commissioners, the court shall accept such finding unless clearly erroneous, and promptly enter an order finding the inmate to be incompetent, staying the execution of the inmate and directing that the inmate be committed to a secure facility under the jurisdiction of the office of mental health if the inmate's incompetency is the result of mental illness. In all other cases, the inmate shall remain in the custody of the department. When an inmate is found competent by a majority of the psychiatric commissioners, the court shall accept such finding unless clearly erroneous, promptly enter an order finding the inmate to be competent and vacating any stay previously issued, and the court shall promptly inform the judge or justice who issued the warrant for the execution of the inmate of the court's finding. Upon being so informed, the judge or justice shall promptly issue a new warrant in accordance with subdivision two of section six hundred fifty of this article. Any other provision of law notwithstanding, no other review, judicial or otherwise, shall be available with respect to an order finding the inmate to be incompetent or competent. If the court rejects the finding of a majority of the psychiatric commissioners on the ground that it is clearly erroneous, the court shall appoint another commission to proceed as provided in this section.

6. When an inmate has been committed to a secure facility pursuant to this section, the inmate shall remain there until the facility administrator determines that the inmate may be competent. Upon so determining, the facility administrator shall promptly notify the court that entered the order finding the inmate to be incompetent, and the court shall promptly notify counsel and the district attorneys and appoint another commission to proceed as provided in this section.

7. The court shall allow reasonable fees to the psychiatric commissioners. The court shall allow reasonable fees for time spent in court and for time reasonably expended out of court to counsel appointed pursuant to this section. The court shall allow all reasonably necessary costs, including without limitation the costs attendant to fees for the examination of the inmate by a qualified psychiatrist or certified psychologist, incurred by the inmate and the district attorney in connection with a petition pursuant to this section. Each claim for compensation and reimbursement shall be supported by a sworn statement specifying the time expended, services

rendered, expenses incurred and reimbursement or compensation applied for or received in the same case from any other source. All such fees and costs shall be a state charge payable on vouchers approved by the court after audit by and on the warrant of the comptroller.

8. When a petition has previously been filed and determined pursuant to this section, the court in which a subsequent petition is filed or to which a subsequent petition is transferred, shall not issue an order staying the execution of the inmate unless the court finds, after notice to the district attorney who prosecuted the inmate and after affording the district attorney a reasonable opportunity to be heard in writing, that there is reasonable cause to believe that the inmate is incompetent; provided, however, that the court may issue an order staying the execution of the inmate, to the extent a stay is necessary to afford the district attorney an opportunity to be heard and such reasonable cause determination to be made.

§ 657.00 Proceeding when person under sentence of death is pregnant.

1. A sentence of death may not be carried out upon a woman while she is pregnant.

2. When the superintendent of the correctional facility where the inmate is confined is informed that reasonable grounds exist that a convicted person under sentence of death may be pregnant, the superintendent shall appoint a qualified physician to examine the convicted person and determine if she is pregnant.

3. Upon being informed by the superintendent that such convicted person is pregnant, the governor shall stay execution of the warrant to the extent necessary.

IV. Execution of Death Sentence

***Comment*:** The execution of a death sentence must be carried out in a way that is valid under both the state and federal Constitutions. The method of execution is of special concern. The Eighth Amendment to the federal Constitution forbids cruel and unusual punishment. The following statue is from New York Correction Law Article 22-B—The Death Penalty. The statute establishes lethal injection as the official method of execution.

§ 658.00 Death penalty inflicted by lethal injection.

The punishment of death shall be inflicted by lethal injection; that is, by the intravenous injection of a substance or substances in a lethal quantity into the body of a person convicted until such person is dead.

V. Sex Offenders

***Comment*:** New York imposes the duty on convicted sex offenders to register with the Division of Criminal Justice Services when they change residences for more than 10 days. They must also notify the division if they attend a place of higher education. The offender must provide a current photograph, current address, and employment information. The following statutes are taken from New York Correction Law.

§ 168-a. Definitions.

As used in this article, the following definitions apply:

1. "Sex offender" includes any person who is convicted of any of the offenses set forth in subdivision two or three of this section. Convictions that result from or are connected with the same act, or result from offenses committed at the same time, shall be counted for the purpose of this article as one conviction. Any conviction set aside pursuant to law is not a conviction for purposes of this article.

2. "Sex offense" means: (a)(i) a conviction of or a conviction for an attempt to commit any of the provisions of sections 130.20, 130.25, 130.30, 130.40, 130.45, 130.60, 250.50, 255.25, 255.26 and 255.27 or article two hundred sixty-three of the penal law, or section 135.05, 135.10, 135.20 or 135.25 of such law relating to kidnapping offenses, provided the victim of such kidnapping or related offense is less than seventeen years old and the offender is not the parent of the victim, or section 230.04, where the person patronized is in fact less than seventeen years of age, 230.05 or 230.06, or subdivision two of section 230.30, or section 230.32 or 230.33 of the penal law, or (ii) a conviction of or a conviction for an attempt to commit any of the provisions of section 235.22 of the penal law, or (iii) a conviction of or a conviction for an attempt to commit any provisions of the foregoing sections committed or attempted as a hate crime defined in section 485.05 of the penal law or as a crime of terrorism defined in section 490.25 of such law; or

(b) a conviction of or a conviction for an attempt to commit any of the provisions of section 130.52 or 130.55 of the penal law, provided the victim of such offense is less than eighteen years of age; or

(c) a conviction of or a conviction for an attempt to commit any of the provisions of section 130.52 or 130.55 of the penal law regardless of the age of the victim and the offender has previously been convicted of: (i) a sex offense defined in this article, (ii) a sexually violent offense defined in this article, or (iii) any of the provisions of section 130.52 or 130.55 of the penal law, or an attempt thereof; or

(d) a conviction of (i) an offense in any other jurisdiction which includes all of the essential elements of any such crime provided for in paragraph (a), (b) or (c) of this subdivision or (ii) a felony in any other jurisdiction for which the offender is required to register as a sex offender in the jurisdiction in which the conviction occurred or, (iii) any of the provisions of 18 U.S.C. 2251, 18 U.S.C. 2251A, 18 U.S.C. 2252, 18 U.S.C. 2252A, or 18 U.S.C. 2260, provided that the elements of such crime of conviction are substantially the same as those which are a part of such offense as of the date on which this subparagraph takes effect.

(e) a conviction of any of the provisions of subdivision two, three or four of section 250.45 of the penal law, unless upon motion by the defendant, the trial court, having regard to the nature and circumstances of the crime and to the history and character of the defendant, is of the opinion that registration would be unduly harsh and inappropriate.

3. "Sexually violent offender" means: (a)(i) a conviction of or a conviction for an attempt to commit any of the provisions of sections 130.35, 130.50, 130.65, 130.66, 130.67, 130.70, 130.75, 130.80, 130.95 and 130.96 of the penal law, or (ii) a conviction of or a conviction for an attempt to commit any of the provisions of sections 130.53, 130.65-a and 130.90 of the penal law, or (iii) a conviction of or a conviction for an attempt to commit any provisions of the

foregoing sections committed or attempted as a hate crime defined in section 485.05 of the penal law or as a crime of terrorism defined in section 490.25 of such law; or

(b) a conviction of an offense in any other jurisdiction which includes all of the essential elements of any such felony provided for in paragraph (a) of this subdivision or conviction of a felony in any other jurisdiction for which the offender is required to register as a sex offender in the jurisdiction in which the conviction occurred.

4. "Law enforcement agency having jurisdiction" means: (a)(i) the chief law enforcement officer in the village, town or city in which the offender expects to reside upon his or her discharge, probation, parole, release to post-release supervision or upon any form of state or local conditional release; or (ii) if there be no chief law enforcement officer in such village, town or city, the chief law enforcement officer of the county in which the offender expects to reside; or (iii) if there be no chief enforcement officer in such village, town, city or county, the division of state police and (b) in the case of a sex offender who is or expects to be employed by, enrolled in, attending or employed, whether for compensation or not, at an institution of higher education, (i) the chief law enforcement officer in the village, town or city in which such institution is located; or (ii) if there be no chief law enforcement officer in such village, town or city, the chief law enforcement officer of the county in which such institution is located; or (iii) if there be no chief law enforcement officer in such village, town, city or county, the division of state police; and (iv) if such institution operates or employs a campus law enforcement or security agency, the chief of such agency.

5. "Division" means the division of criminal justice services as defined by section eight hundred thirty-seven of the executive law.

6. "Hospital" means a hospital as defined in subdivision two of section four hundred of this chapter and applies to persons committed to such hospital by order of commitment made pursuant to article sixteen of this chapter.

7. (a) "Sexual predator" means a sex offender who has been convicted of a sexually violent offense defined in subdivision three of this section and who suffers from a mental abnormality or personality disorder that makes him or her likely to engage in predatory sexually violent offenses.

(b) "Sexually violent offender" means a sex offender who has been convicted of a sexually violent offense defined in subdivision three of this section.

(c) "Predicate sex offender" means a sex offender who has been convicted of an offense set forth in subdivision two or three of this section when the offender has been previously convicted of an offense set forth in subdivision two or three of this section.

8. "Mental abnormality" means a congenital or acquired condition of a person that affects the emotional or volitional capacity of the person in a manner that predisposes that person to the commission of criminal sexual acts to a degree that makes the person a menace to the health and safety of other persons.

9. "Predatory" means an act directed at a stranger, or a person with whom a relationship has been established or promoted for the primary purpose of victimization.

10. "Board" means the "board of examiners of sex offenders" established pursuant to section one hundred sixty-eight-l of this article.

11. "Local correctional facility" means a local correctional facility as that term is defined in subdivision sixteen of section two of this chapter.

12. Probation means a sentence of probation imposed pursuant to article sixty-five of the penal law and shall include a sentence of imprisonment imposed in conjunction with a sentence of probation.

13. "Institution of higher education" means an institution in the state providing higher education as such term is defined in subdivision eight of section two of the education law.

14. "Nonresident worker" means any person required to register as a sex offender in another jurisdiction who is employed or carries on a vocation in this state, on either a full-time or a part-time basis, with or without compensation, for more than fourteen consecutive days, or for an aggregate period exceeding thirty days in a calendar year.

15. "Nonresident student" means a person required to register as a sex offender in another jurisdiction who is enrolled on a full-time or part-time basis in any public or private educational institution in this state including any secondary school, trade or professional institution or institution of higher education.

§ 168-f. Duty to register and to verify.

1. Any sex offender shall, (a) at least ten calendar days prior to discharge, parole, release to post-release supervision or release from any state or local correctional facility, hospital or institution where he or she was confined or committed, or, (b) at the time sentence is imposed for any sex offender released on probation or discharged upon payment of a fine, conditional discharge or unconditional discharge, register with the division on a form prepared by the division.

2. For a sex offender required to register under this article on each anniversary of the sex offender's initial registration date during the period in which he is required to register under this section the following applies:

(a) The sex offender shall mail the verification form to the division within ten calendar days after receipt of the form.

(b) The verification form shall be signed by the sex offender, and state that he still resides at the address last reported to the division.

(b-1) If the sex offender has been given a level three designation, such offender shall sign the verification form, and state that he or she still is employed at the address last reported to the division.

(b-2) If the sex offender has been given a level three designation, he or she shall personally appear at the law enforcement agency having jurisdiction within twenty days of the first anniversary of the sex offender's initial registration and every year thereafter during the period of registration for the purpose of providing a current photograph of such offender. The law enforcement agency having jurisdiction shall photograph the sex offender and shall promptly forward a copy of such photograph to the division. For purposes of this paragraph, if such sex offender is confined in a state or local correctional facility, the local law enforcement agency having jurisdiction shall be the warden, superintendent, sheriff or other person in charge of the state or local correctional facility.

(b-3) If the sex offender has been given a level one or level two designation, he or she shall personally appear at the law enforcement agency having jurisdiction within twenty days of the third anniversary of the sex offender's initial registration and every three years thereafter during the period of registration for the purpose of providing a current photograph of such offender. The law enforcement agency having jurisdiction shall photograph the sex offender and shall promptly forward a copy of such photograph to the division. For purposes of this paragraph, if such sex offender is confined in a state or local correctional facility, the local law enforcement agency having jurisdiction shall be the warden, superintendent, sheriff or other person in charge of the state or local correctional facility.

(c) If the sex offender fails to mail the signed verification form to the division within ten calendar days after receipt of the form, he or she shall be in violation of this section unless he proves that he or she has not changed his or her residence address.

(c-1) If the sex offender, to whom a notice has been mailed at the last reported address pursuant to paragraph b of subdivision one of section one hundred sixty-eight-b of this article, fails to personally appear at the law enforcement agency having jurisdiction, as provided in paragraph (b-2) or (b-3) of this subdivision, within twenty days of the anniversary of the sex offender's initial registration, or an alternate later date scheduled by the law enforcement agency having jurisdiction, he or she shall be in violation of this section. The duty to personally appear for such updated photograph shall be temporarily suspended during any period in which the sex offender is confined in any hospital or institution, and such sex offender shall personally appear for such updated photograph no later than ninety days after release from such hospital or institution, or an alternate later date scheduled by the law enforcement agency having jurisdiction.

3. The provisions of subdivision two of this section shall be applied to a sex offender required to register under this article except that such sex offender designated as a sexual predator or having been given a level three designation must personally verify his or her address with the local law enforcement agency every ninety calendar days after the date of release or commencement of parole or post-release supervision, or probation, or release on payment of a fine, conditional discharge or unconditional discharge. The duty to personally verify shall be temporarily suspended during any period in which the sex offender is confined to any state or local correctional facility, hospital or institution and shall immediately recommence on the date of the sex offender's release.

4. Any sex offender shall register with the division no later than ten calendar days after any change of address or any change of his or her status of enrollment, attendance, employment or residence at any institution of higher education. A fee of ten dollars, as authorized by subdivision eight of section one hundred sixty-eight-b of this article, shall be submitted by the sex offender each time such offender registers any change of address or any change of his or her status of enrollment, attendance, employment or residence at any institution of higher education. Any failure or omission to submit the required fee shall not affect the acceptance by the division of the change of address or change of status.

5. The duty to register under the provisions of this article shall not be applicable to any sex offender whose conviction was reversed upon appeal or who was pardoned by the governor.

6. Any nonresident worker or nonresident student, as defined in subdivisions fourteen and fifteen of section one hundred sixty-eight-a of this article, shall register his or her current address and

the address of his or her place of employment or educational institution attended with the division within ten calendar days after such nonresident worker or nonresident student commences employment or attendance at an educational institution in the state. Any nonresident worker or nonresident student shall notify the division of any change of residence, employment or educational institution address no later than ten days after such change. The division shall notify the law enforcement agency where the nonresident worker is employed or the educational institution is located that a nonresident worker or nonresident student is present in that agency's jurisdiction.

§ 168-h. Duration of registration and verification.

1. The duration of registration and verification for a sex offender who has not been designated a sexual predator, or a sexually violent offender, or a predicate sex offender, and who is classified as a level one risk, or who has not yet received a risk level classification, shall be annually for a period of twenty years from the initial date of registration.

2. The duration of registration and verification for a sex offender who, on or after March eleventh, two thousand two, is designated a sexual predator, or a sexually violent offender, or a predicate sex offender, or who is classified as a level two or level three risk, shall be annually for life. Notwithstanding the foregoing, a sex offender who is classified as a level two risk and who is not designated a sexual predator, a sexually violent offender or a predicate sex offender, may be relieved of the duty to register and verify as provided by subdivision one of section one hundred sixty-eight-o of this article.

3. Any sex offender having been designated a level three risk or a sexual predator shall also personally verify his or her address every ninety calendar days with the local law enforcement agency having jurisdiction where the offender resides.

§ 168-j. Notification of local law enforcement agencies of change of address.

1. Upon receipt of a change of address by a sex offender required to register under this article, the division shall notify the local law enforcement agency having jurisdiction of the new place of residence and the local law enforcement agency where the sex offender last resided of the new place of residence.

2. Upon receipt of change of address information, the local law enforcement agency having jurisdiction of the new place of residence shall adhere to the notification provisions set forth in subdivision six of section one hundred sixty-eight-l of this article.

3. The division shall, if the sex offender changes residence to another state, notify the appropriate agency within that state of the new place of residence.

4. Upon receipt of a change in the status of the enrollment, attendance, employment or residence at an institution of higher education by a sex offender required to register under this article, the division shall notify each law enforcement agency having jurisdiction which is affected by such change.

5. Upon receipt of change in the status of the enrollment, attendance, employment or residence at an institution of higher education by a sex offender required to register under this article, each

law enforcement agency having jurisdiction shall adhere to the notification provisions set forth in subdivision six of section one hundred sixty-eight-l of this article.

§ 168-t. Penalty.

Any sex offender required to register or to verify pursuant to the provisions of this article who fails to register or verify in the manner and within the time periods provided for herein or who violates the provisions of section one hundred sixty-eight-v of this article shall be guilty of a class A misdemeanor upon conviction for the first offense, and upon conviction for a second or subsequent offense shall be guilty of a class D felony. Any such failure to register or verify may also be the basis for revocation of parole pursuant to section two hundred fifty-nine-I of the executive law or the basis for revocation of probation pursuant to article four hundred ten of the criminal procedure law.

Questions

1. Ted is convicted of a traffic violation. What is the maximum number of days he can be imprisoned for?

2. Name the three categories of misdemeanors.

3. What are three mitigating factors set out in statute that can be considered by a jury in a death penalty case?

4. Betty is a registered sex offender. When she was a teacher, she was convicted of indecent solicitation of a child after she attempted to lure a male student to her home. Since then, she has received two years of treatment. She moves across town to a new apartment. How long does she have before she must inform the division of her move?

5. Todd is a registered sex offender, and has been classified as a sexual predator. After he is released from prison, how long will he have to stay registered with the Division of Criminal Justice Services?

6. Hank is convicted of first-degree murder, for killing a witness who was going to testify at the trial of a mob boss. Can Hank be sentenced to death?